G000123285

AWESOME CAKES FOR Kids

THE AUSTRALIAN WOMEN'S WEEKLY

TRIPLE TESTED

TEST KITCHEN

THE AUSTRALIAN **Women's Weekly**

AWESOME CAKES FOR *Kids*

INCLUDES
PUZZLES
& GAMES
+ CRAFT

OVER
140
CAKES

CONTENTS

LET THEM Eat Cake

This is an amazing collection of cakes for kids, but some kids just never grow up – so why not make use of some of these brilliant ideas for cakes for those grown-up kids too!

Most of the INGREDIENTS USED IN THIS BOOK COME FROM SUPERMARKETS, MAKING THE SHOPPING AS EASY AS POSSIBLE FOR THE CAKE-MAKER. IN JUST A FEW CASES, DECORATIONS HAVE BEEN BOUGHT ONLINE, OR AT SHOPS THAT SPECIALISE IN CAKE DECORATING EQUIPMENT. THERE IS AN INCREDIBLE AMOUNT OF WONDERFUL DECORATIONS AND INFORMATION TO BE FOUND ONLINE.

THROUGHOUT THE BOOK THERE ARE HELPFUL HINTS AND TIPS FOR EACH CAKE AND, AT THE BACK OF THE BOOK, THERE'S LOADS OF INFORMATION AND STEP BY STEP PHOTOS TO HELP BOTH THE BEGINNER AND ADVANCED CAKE-MAKER. IT'S A GOOD IDEA TO READ THIS BEFORE STARTING TO MAKE A CAKE.

Kids love these books – they usually become part of their must-read library at bedtime, especially as the big day gets closer. The hard part for the cake-maker is trying to convince an excited child that it's perfectly fine to change the colour of a cake or even some of the decorations – good luck with that – most kids want an exact replica of the cake in the book.

The best way to tackle a cake is to first nail down the decision on the cake, get the ingredients in and hidden well away at least a week before the party, a little longer if items have been ordered online.

Bake or buy the base cake at least a day before the party, or make it well in advance and freeze it. If butter cream is being used, make it, colour it (colours change on standing), cover it and leave it to stand at a cool room temperature for at least four hours before use – up to 12 hours is fine too, providing the weather isn't too hot. Don't refrigerate the butter cream if it can be avoided, as the ingredients will almost certainly split when stirred or beaten. If you must refrigerate it, allow the butter cream to return to room temperature before stirring.

AFTER CUTTING THE CAKE TO SHAPE, CHILL OR PARTLY FREEZE IT BEFORE FROSTING, THEN THE FUN BEGINS WITH THE DECORATIONS AND LOLLIES. THE REAL REWARD COMES WHEN THE BIRTHDAY CHILD SEES THE FINISHED CAKE.

WHEN I grow up

TIPS

We used red food colouring gel for this recipe to get an intense colour. If using a liquid colouring you may need to add some icing sugar to stop the frosting from splitting.

EMERGENCY RESPONSE
FIRE SQUAD

1 Secure one of the slab cakes on cake board with a little frosting. Spread cake with a little frosting then top with remaining slab cake. Using a serrated knife, cut the round cake in half to form two semi-circles. Sandwich semi-circles together with a little frosting. Using picture as a guide, secure semi-circle cake with a little frosting next to slab cake, on the board.

2 Trim edges of two doughnuts so they sit flat on their sides. Using picture as a guide, attach doughnuts to the sides and on top of the cake with a little frosting.

3 Tint frosting red. Spread frosting over top and sides of cake.

4 Using scissors, cut licorice strap into 25cm (10-inch) and 35cm (14-inch) lengths. Using picture as a guide, position licorice on cake. Position fruit rings on cake.

5 Knead ready-made icing on a surface dusted with a little sifted icing sugar until icing loses its stickiness. Roll icing into a 45cm (18-inch) long rope. Using picture as a guide, position the yellow rope, ice-cream cone, blue sanding sugar and stars around cake.

EQUIPMENT
- 30CM X 40XM (12-INCH X 16-INCH) RECTANGULAR CAKE BOARD (PAGE 332)

CAKE
- 1 X 450G (14½-OUNCE) PACKET DOUBLE UNFILLED SPONGE SLABS
- 2 X 453G (14½-OUNCE) TUBS VANILLA FROSTING
- ½ X 460G (14½-OUNCE) PACKET DOUBLE UNFILLED SPONGE CAKE ROUND (YOU NEED 1 CAKE)
- 3 CINNAMON DOUGHNUTS
- RED FOOD COLOURING GEL

DECORATIONS
- 60CM (24-INCH) PIECE BLACK LICORICE STRAP
- 3 YELLOW FRUIT RINGS
- 1 RED FRUIT RING
- 125G (4 OUNCES) READY-MADE YELLOW ICING
- PURE ICING (CONFECTIONERS') SUGAR, FOR DUSTING
- 1 ICE-CREAM CONE
- ¼ CUP BLUE SANDING SUGAR
- ¼ CUP BLUE STAR SPRINKLES

DOING THE RIGHT THING

EQUIPMENT

- 20CM (8-INCH) SQUARE CAKE BOARD (PAGE 332)

CAKE

- 2 X 450G (14½-OUNCE) PACKAGED DOUBLE UNFILLED SPONGE SLABS
- 2 QUANTITIES BUTTER CREAM (PAGE 327)
- RED FOOD COLOURING

DECORATIONS

- 3 WHITE MILK BOTTLES
- 4 COLA BOTTLES
- 4 BLUE SPRINKLE LICORICE ALLSORTS
- 10 ASSORTED COLOURED M&M'S
- 4 JELLY SNAKES
- 2 RED LICORICE TUBES
- ½ X 240G (7½-OUNCE) PACKET BLACK LICORICE STRAPS
- 2 RED M&M'S

1 Sandwich three sponges together upright with a little butter cream. Use a serrated knife to trim two long sides of cake into a wheelie bin shape (make the top edge into a 12cm (4¾-inch) square and the bottom edge 11cm (4½-inch) square.

2 Secure cake onto the cake board with a little butter cream. Tint remaining butter cream red; spread three-quarters of the butter cream over the top and sides of cake.

3 Position milk bottles, cola bottles, licorice allsorts, M&M's and jelly snakes over top of cake.

4 Use a serrated knife to trim remaining sponge into a 12cm (4¾-inch) square. Split cake in half; spread remaining butter cream all over top, sides and base of one cake. (Reserve remaining cake for another use).

5 Place the cake at an angle over the top of the lollies to create a lid; secure licorice tubes to the top to form handles.

6 Unroll each licorice strap until you are left with a 4cm (1½-inch) round; trim away unrolled pieces. Cut licorice rounds in half through the centre to make two wheels. Position wheels on cake; secure red M&M's to centre of wheels with a little butter cream.

TIPS We've use a mixture of lollies to turn this into a rubbish bin. To make this a recycle bin, use a variety of milk bottles. Save any licorice off-cuts for another use.

TIPS

Pink and orange nerds are found in neon nerds. Black cats and white milk bottles can be found in packets of party mix.

GONE FISHING

1 Preheat oven to 180°C/350°F. Grease cake pan; line base with baking paper. Line 4 holes of muffin pan with paper cases.

2 Make cakes according to directions on packets. Drop 3 level teaspoons of the mixture into paper cases; bake about 15 minutes. Pour remaining mixture into round cake pan; bake about 40 minutes. Stand cakes in pans 5 minutes before turning, top-side up, onto wire racks to cool.

3 Using a serrated knife, level top of large cake; turn cake cut-side down. Cut cake into a fishbowl shape; secure on board with a little butter cream.

4 Place two-thirds of the butter cream in a small bowl; tint blue. Place half the remaining butter cream in a small bowl, keep plain. Place half the remaining butter cream in a small bowl; tint orange. Tint remaining butter cream green.

5 Using picture as a guide, spread blue butter cream over the top and sides of the cake to make water. Spread plain butter cream over the top of the cake, as pictured, reserving 1 tablespoon.

6 Spread orange butter cream over the top of two muffins; spread green butter cream over the top of one muffin. Spread remaining muffin with reserved plain butter cream. Using picture as a guide, decorate cupcakes with sprinkles. Position cupcakes on fishbowl.

7 Position nerds on one orange cake and green cake to resemble eyes. Position half a green sour jelly bean on other orange cake to resemble eye. Cut the top from one milk bottle, place on green cake for fin. Cut Aero Bar into two 1cm (½-inch) slices; position on green cake for tail. Trim red jubes and black cat to resemble fins and tails; position on orange cakes.

8 Using picture as a guide, slice jelly baby and milk bottles, lengthways, into strips; alternate cut sides to make striped fish, position on white cake. Trim yellow jube; position for fin and tail. Position a halved pink sour jelly bean for eyes. Decorate fishbowl with sour jelly beans and trimmed jelly snakes.

EQUIPMENT

- DEEP 30CM (12-INCH) ROUND CAKE PAN
- 12-HOLE (1-TABLESPOON/ 20ML) MINI MUFFIN PAN
- 4 MINI MUFFIN PAPER CASES
- 35CM (14-INCH) SQUARE CAKE BOARD (PAGE 332)

CAKE

- 5 X 340G (11-OUNCE) PACKETS BUTTER CAKE MIX
- 2 QUANTITIES BUTTER CREAM (PAGE 327)
- BLUE, ORANGE AND GREEN FOOD COLOURING

DECORATIONS

- ORANGE SPRINKLES
- YELLOW SPRINKLES
- 1 EACH PINK AND ORANGE NERDS
- ½ X 190G (6-OUNCE) PACKET SOUR JELLY BEANS
- 2 WHITE MILK BOTTLES
- ¼ X 40G (1½-OUNCE) PEPPERMINT AERO BAR
- 2 RED JUBES
- 1 JELLY BLACK CAT
- 1 CHOCOLATE JELLY BABY
- 1 YELLOW JUBE
- 5 GREEN JELLY SNAKES

LOLLIPOP CAKES

1 Preheat oven to 160°C/325°F. Line muffin pan with paper cases.

2 Make cake according to directions on packet. Drop 1 tablespoon of the mixture into each case; bake about 20 minutes. Stand cakes in pan 5 minutes before turning, top-side up, onto a wire rack to cool.

3 Line flower pots with pieces of baking paper; place cakes in pots (see tips).

4 Tint butter cream pale green, spoon into piping bag; pipe icing onto each cake.

5 Sprinkle cakes with sugar sprinkles. Push a lollipop into the centre; position jubes as leaves.

EQUIPMENT

- **12-HOLE (1-TABLESPOON/20ML) MINI MUFFIN PAN**
- **12 MINI MUFFIN PAN CASES**
- **12 SPROUTING BEAUTY FLOWER POTS (SEE TIPS)**
- **PIPING BAG FITTED WITH A SMALL STAR PIPING TUBE**

CAKE

- **1 X 340G (11-OUNCE) PACKET CHOCOLATE CAKE MIX**
- **½ QUANTITY BUTTER CREAM (PAGE 327)**
- **GREEN FOOD COLOURING**

DECORATION

- **GREEN SUGAR SPRINKLES**
- **12 LOLLIPOPS**
- **12 GREEN DIAMOND-SHAPED JUBES, HALVED**

TIPS

Sprouting beauty flower pots are available from leading hardware stores. If the cakes sink below the top of the flower pots, screw up some baking paper and line the base of the pot to give added height. There will be cake mix left over, so make extra cakes for the party guests.

TIP
Store in an airtight container at a cool room temperature until ready to serve.

CLOWN CAKE POPS

1 Using a fork, combine cake crumbs and jam in a small bowl. Shape level tablespoons of mixture into balls, squeezing firmly. Place balls on a baking paper-lined tray; freeze 1 hour or refrigerate 3 hours or overnight until firm.

2 Melt white chocolate (page 337). Pour into a heatproof jug. Dip the end of one lollipop stick into chocolate, then push it about halfway into a ball of cake. Return to tray. Repeat with remaining sticks and cake balls. Freeze 5 minutes to set.

3 Re-melt white chocolate, if necessary. Dip a cake pop into the chocolate, rocking back and forth to coat (don't swirl the pop as it'll break). Allow excess chocolate to drip back into jug. Stand cake pop upright in a styrofoam block until set. Repeat with remaining cake pops. Re-melt chocolate as required.

4 Tint leftover melted white chocolate blue. Carefully trim 4.5cm (1¾-inch)

from the wide end of the cones, discard trimmings. Dip the edge of the cone in blue-coloured chocolate. Place cone on top of a cake pop to make the clown's hat; working quickly attach nerds. Hold in place for about a minute or until just set. Repeat with the remaining cones, chocolate and nerds. Attach gobstoppers to top of hats with a little melted chocolate. Stand upright until set.

5 Spoon royal icing into paper piping bag, snip a small opening in the tip. Using royal icing, secure Jaffas as noses, and secure a piece of sliced raspberries to form the mouth. Secure two pieces of jelly beans on each clown for rosy cheeks.

6 Using a small sharp knife, cut small crosses from licorice; secure with royal icing to form eyes. Thread 5 cupcake cases onto sticks to form clown's collar.

EQUIPMENT

- 10 LOLLIPOP OR ICE-CREAM STICKS
- STYROFOAM BLOCK OR EGG CARTON
- PAPER PIPING BAG (PAGE 336)

CAKE

- 1¼ CUPS (220G) FIRMLY PACKED MADEIRA OR BUTTER CAKE CRUMBS
- 2 TEASPOONS STRAWBERRY JAM (CONSERVE)
- 300G (9½ OUNCES) WHITE CHOCOLATE MELTS
- BLUE FOOD COLOURING SUITABLE FOR CHOCOLATE
- ¼ QUANTITY ROYAL ICING (PAGE 327)

DECORATIONS

- 10 MINI ICE-CREAM CONES
- 2 TABLESPOONS EACH GRAPE, ORANGE AND PINK NERDS, COMBINED
- 10 GOBSTOPPERS
- 10 JAFFAS
- 2 JELLY RASPBERRIES, SLICED THINLY
- 5 PINK JELLY BEANS, HALVED CROSSWAYS
- 10CM (4-INCH) PIECE BLACK LICORICE STRAP
- 50 FOIL CUPCAKE CASES

SURF'S UP
LITTLE DUDE

EQUIPMENT

- 1 MEDIUM ZIPTOP PLASTIC BAG
- OVEN TRAY
- SMALL PALETTE KNIFE
- 30CM X 45CM (12-INCH X 18-INCH) RECTANGULAR CAKE BOARD (PAGE 332)
- 1 LARGE ZIPTOP PLASTIC BAG

CAKE

- 1 X 450G (14½-OUNCE) PACKET DOUBLE UNFILLED SPONGE SLABS
- 1 X 453G (14½-OUNCE) TUB VANILLA FROSTING
- BLUE FOOD COLOURING GEL

DECORATIONS

- 50G (1½ OUNCES) WHITE CHOCOLATE MELTS
- ORANGE FOOD COLOURING SUITABLE FOR CHOCOLATE
- 1 RED FRUIT RING
- 1 LARGE WAFFLE ICE-CREAM CONE
- 250G (8 OUNCES) PLAIN SWEET BISCUITS
- 2 RAINBOW SOUR STRAPS
- 2 SMALL WOODEN SKEWERS
- 1 LICORICE ALLSORT, GREEN LAYER ONLY
- 1 YELLOW BOOTLACE

1 Melt chocolate (page 337). Reserve 1 tablespoon of the chocolate. Tint remaining chocolate orange. Pour orange chocolate into medium ziptop bag, snip one corner from bag. Using the template as a guide (page 338), pipe surfboards onto oven tray lined with baking paper, quickly spread with a palette knife to smooth surface. Leave to set. Drizzle reserved white chocolate over fruit ring to create a float.

2 Secure cakes, long sides together, on cake board with a little frosting. Tint half the remaining frosting blue. Using picture as a guide, spread all but 1 tablespoon of the plain frosting over one-third of the cake. Spread blue frosting over remaining cake and ice-cream cone. Position cone on top of cake to make wave. Using tip of palette knife, swirl some of the reserved plain frosting on top and around cone to create the wave breaks.

3 Seal biscuits in large ziptop bag; gently pound with a rolling pin or meat mallet until crushed. Sprinkle biscuit crumbs over plain frosting and around edge of cake to resemble sand.

4 Using kitchen scissors cut green and blue section from one of the sour straps. Place on one of the surfboards; trim to fit. Cut remaining red and yellow section into two 3cm x 5cm (1¼-inch x 2-inch) flags. Thread each flag onto the end of a skewer. Push flags into cake. Cut green layer of licorice allsort into a star; secure onto one of the surfboards with a little frosting.

5 Cut remaining sour strap into 2 x 5cm (2-inch) towels. Using picture as a guide, position surfboards, bootlace, towels and float on sand.

HAPPY BIRTHDAY
CHALK BOARD

1 To make chalk board, knead ready-made black icing on a surface dusted with a little sifted icing sugar until icing loses its stickiness. Roll icing between two sheets of baking paper until 2mm (⅛-inch) thick. Cut into a 22cm x 27cm (8¾-inch x 10¾-inch) rectangle. Stand icing overnight to dry.

2 Turn two of the cakes top-side down; secure, long sides together, on cake board with a little frosting. Spread tops with a little frosting. Top with remaining cakes. Reserve 2 tablespoons of the frosting for decorating. Spread remaining frosting over top and sides of cake. Top cake with chalk board.

3 Knead ready-made red and green icings, separately, on a surface dusted with a little sifted icing sugar until icing loses its stickiness. Roll each piece on a surface dusted with a little icing sugar until 2mm (⅛-inch) thick. Cut red icing into an apple shape; cut green icing into a leaf shape. Secure to chalk board with a little water.

4 Secure licorice sticks around the edge of chalk board with a little frosting, trimming to fit. Draw on chalk board with chalk.

YOU NEED TO MAKE THE CHALK BOARD THE DAY BEFORE AS IT MUST DRY OVERNIGHT.

EQUIPMENT
- 30CM X 40XM (12-INCH X 16-INCH) RECTANGULAR CAKE BOARD (PAGE 332)

CAKE
- 2 X 450G (14½-OUNCE) PACKETS DOUBLE UNFILLED SPONGE SLABS
- ½ X 453G (14½-OUNCE) TUB CHOCOLATE FROSTING

DECORATIONS
- 3 X 125G (4-OUNCE) PACKETS READY-MADE BLACK ICING
- PURE ICING (CONFECTIONERS') SUGAR, FOR DUSTING
- 30G (1 OUNCE) READY-MADE RED ICING
- 15G (½ OUNCE) READY-MADE GREEN ICING
- 7 CHOCOLATE-COATED LICORICE STICKS
- NON-TOXIC CHALK

PRIMA BALLERINA

EQUIPMENT

- HOT GLUE GUN OR CRAFT GLUE
- 30CM (12-INCH) ROUND CAKE BOARD (PAGE 332)

CAKE

- 1 X 460G (14½-OUNCE) PACKET DOUBLE UNFILLED SPONGE CAKE ROUNDS
- 1 X 453G (14½-OUNCE) TUB VANILLA FROSTING
- PINK FOOD COLOURING

DECORATIONS

- 1 SMALL FANCY DRESS PINK TUTU
- 60CM X 3.5CM (2-FEET X 1½-INCH) PINK RIBBON
- 30CM (12 INCHES) THIN PINK RIBBON
- 2 WHITE MILK BOTTLES
- 1 PRINCESS CROWN (TIARA)

1 Using glue gun, glue tutu to cake board; stand 1 hour to dry.

2 Spread one cake with ½ cup frosting and top with remaining cake. Place on a piece of baking paper, cut a little smaller than cake. Tint frosting pink; spread over top and sides of cake. Carefully place cake over tutu on board.

3 Tie 60cm ribbon around cake; secure ends together with a little glue. Tie strips of thin ribbon around milk bottles to make ballet slippers, as pictured; position next to cake. Top cake with crown.

TIP We bought the tutu from a discount store.

OLYMPIC CHAMPION
BEST BIRTHDAY EVER

1 Melt chocolate (page 337). To make gold medal, working quickly, dip one wagon wheel in chocolate to coat, drain off excess; cover both sides with gold shimmer. Repeat with remaining wagon wheels, melted chocolate, silver shimmer and orange sprinkles to make silver and bronze medals. Stand at room temperature until set. Cut ice-cream wafer in half; spread chocolate over one side of wafer, stand until set. Discard remaining wafer half.

2 Trim cakes; secure two of the cakes, long sides together, on cake board with a little frosting. Spread frosting over top and sides of cake.

3 To make podium, cut remaining cake into 6 squares.

4 Using a little frosting, secure three squares on top of each other to make gold medal podium. Repeat with two squares to make silver podium. Leave third square as is for bronze podium. Spread frosting all over squares.

5 Using picture as a guide, carefully position podiums on cake. Wrap 6 of the sour straps around side of cake, cutting to fit; secure with a little frosting, if necessary.

6 Cut remaining sour strap into 3 pieces to represent ribbons; cut 'V' shape in one end of each strap. Position ribbons on each podium.

7 Push a skewer into centre of each podium, making sure to push all the way down to cake board. Position medals on podiums, leaning up against skewers, trim skewers as necessary, so they are hidden behind the medals. Use the writing icings to draw olympic rings on the wafer; position in front of podium.

EQUIPMENT
- 30CM X 45CM (12-INCH X 18-INCH) RECTANGULAR CAKE BOARD (PAGE 332)
- WOODEN SKEWERS

CAKE
- 1½ X 450G (14½-OUNCE) PACKAGED DOUBLE UNFILLED SPONGE SLABS (3 CAKES TOTAL)
- 1 X 453G (14½-OUNCE) TUB VANILLA FROSTING

DECORATIONS
- 150G (4½ OUNCES) WHITE CHOCOLATE MELTS
- 3 MINI WAGON WHEELS
- 2 TABLESPOONS EDIBLE GOLD SHIMMER POWDER
- 2 TABLESPOONS EDIBLE SILVER SHIMMER POWDER
- 2 TABLESPOONS ORANGE SPRINKLES, CRUSHED
- 1 ICE-CREAM WAFER
- 7 RAINBOW SOUR STRAPS
- BLUE, YELLOW, BLACK, GREEN AND RED WRITING ICINGS

I WANNA BE A POP STAR

EQUIPMENT

- 30CM (12-INCH) ROUND CAKE BOARD (PAGE 332)

CAKE

- 2 X 460G (14½-OUNCE) PACKETS DOUBLE UNFILLED SPONGE CAKE ROUNDS
- 2 X 453G (14½-OUNCE) TUBS VANILLA FROSTING

DECORATIONS

- 10 ICE-CREAM CONES
- 220G (7 OUNCES) WHITE CHOCOLATE, CHOPPED
- EDIBLE SILVER SHIMMER POWDER
- 1 CUP GREEN SPRINKLES
- 1M (1 YARD) BLACK LICORICE STRAP
- 1 RED SOUR FRUIT RING
- 4 YELLOW TICTOC BISCUITS

1 Process two of the cakes into crumbs. Using a fork, combine crumbs and ¼ cup of the frosting in a medium bowl. Roll ¼-cups of mixture into 10 balls. Place on an oven tray, loosely cover with plastic wrap. Refrigerate 2 hours or until firm.

2 Stand ice-cream cones upright in a wire rack. Melt chocolate (page 337). Dip cake balls into chocolate, allowing any excess chocolate to drip off. Position balls in ice-cream cones; allow to set for a few minutes then roll in silver shimmer. Stand until completely set.

3 Secure one of the remaining cakes to the cake board with a little frosting; spread top with ½ cup of the frosting, then top with remaining cake. Spread sides only of cake with frosting. Place sprinkles on a lipped oven tray; roll cake on its side to cover in sprinkles. Spread top of cake with remaining frosting.

4 Using scissors; cut 65cm of the licorice strap into a thin 2mm (⅛-inch) thick strip. Place around the top edge of cake, as pictured. Cut two 10cm (4-inch) thin strips of licorice from leftover 65cm strap.

5 Trim point off the base of two ice-cream cones. Place cones on top of cake with 10cm licorice strips sticking out of the bottom of the cones as electrical cords. Arrange the remaining ice-cream cones around cake on board, if you like. Secure fruit ring to the side of cake with a little frosting.

6 To make headphones, cut remaining licorice strap into a 20cm (8-inch) piece. Split leftover licorice lengthways into two pieces (discard one piece). Using picture as a guide, position one end of thin strap into fruit ring to form the cord linking cake to the headphones. Split the top end of the strap lengthways in half so it can go into the ears of the headphones.

7 Use a little frosting to sandwich biscuits together, yellow-side out. Using picture as a guide, sandwich licorice pieces between biscuits to complete the headphones. Decorate the sides of the headphones with 'volume control', if you like (we cut a piece of licorice allsort into a circle and attached to the biscuit with a little frosting).

ARTIST'S PAINT
PALETTE

1 Secure two of the cakes, long sides together, on cake board with a little frosting. Spread top with a little frosting. Top with remaining cakes. Spread top and sides of cake with a quarter of the frosting.

2 Divide remaining frosting into 4 small bowls. Tint each bowl a different colour.

3 Melt chocolate (page 337). Attach two mini sponge rolls together with a little of the melted chocolate. Trim one end to shape into a paint tube. Repeat with remaining sponge rolls. Spread each tube with some of the different coloured frosting.

4 Cut wafer into 4 rectangles. Spread wafers with remaining chocolate. Allow to set.

5 Place remaining coloured frosting into piping bags. Snip the end off piping bags. Pipe a heart shape onto each wafer. Position wafers onto paint tubes.

6 Using picture as a guide, position M&M's, paint tubes and ice-cream cones on cake.

7 Write a party message onto cake with frosting. Cut licorice strap into a round to fit the opening of one ice-cream cone. Secure with a little chocolate to make lid. Cut a larger hole at end of piping bags. Pipe frosting coming out of remaining ice-cream cones.

EQUIPMENT
- 35CM X 45CM (14-INCH X 18-INCH) RECTANGULAR CAKE BOARD (PAGE 332)
- 4 DISPOSABLE PLASTIC PIPING BAGS

CAKE
- 2 X 450G (14½-OUNCE) PACKETS DOUBLE UNFILLED SPONGE SLABS
- 2 X 453G (14½-OUNCE) TUBS VANILLA FROSTING
- BLUE, RED, GREEN AND YELLOW FOOD COLOURING

DECORATIONS
- 50G (1½ OUNCES) WHITE CHOCOLATE MELTS
- 8 MINI SPONGE ROLLS
- 1 ICE-CREAM WAFER
- 65 M&M'S
- 4 ICE-CREAM CONES, ENDS TRIMMED
- 2CM (¾-INCH) PIECE BLACK LICORICE STRAP

DOCTORS
WITHOUT BORDERS

EQUIPMENT
- 30CM (12-INCH) SQUARE CAKE BOARD (PAGE 332)

CAKE
- 1 X 450G (14½-OUNCE) PACKETS DOUBLE UNFILLED SPONGE SLABS
- 1½ X 453G (14½-OUNCE) TUBS VANILLA FROSTING

DECORATIONS
- 10 PLAIN ICE-CREAM WAFERS
- 3 RED SOUR STRAPS
- BLACK LICORICE STRAP
- 6 WHITE MARSHMALLOWS
- 1 X TIC TOC BISCUIT
- 12 PEPPERMINT LOLLIES
- 1 X 290G PACKET JELLY RASPBERRIES
- 1 X 49G CONTAINER WHITE TIC TAC PEPPERMINTS
- 1 X 29G CONTAINER BLUE TIC TAC POWERMINTS
- 2 TABLESPOONS BLUE MINI M&M'S
- ½ CUP BLUE M&M'S
- SMALL PLASTIC JARS AND BOWLS

1 Sandwich cakes together, upright on long sides, with a little frosting. Secure to cake board with a little frosting. Spread frosting all over cake.

2 Using picture as a guide, position one wafer on centre top of bag to form a strap; cut another wafer in half and position pieces on front and back of bag to complete strap. Cut thin strips of sour strap and position around wafer edges. Cut one strap into a cross shape, secure to wafer with a little frosting.

3 Cut 5 wafers in half crossways; cut each half diagonally into 4 triangles. Secure triangles on edges of bag, as pictured. Cut a piece of licorice strap and push into top of bag to form the handle.

4 To make stethoscope, cut a 40cm (16 inch) piece of licorice strap; split in half, making a 15cm (6 inch) split at one end. Position half a marshmallow on each end for ear buds. Spread frosting over biscuit. Cut a piece of sour strap into

a heart shape and attach to biscuit, as pictured.

5 Sandwich 4 wafers together with a little frosting; cover top of wafer with frosting to make a prescription pad. Cut sour strap to make a cross shape and secure to top of prescription pad.

6 Position remaining marshmallows in a pile to form cotton balls. Place remaining lollies in jars and bottles; position around cake to make pills and medicines.

TIPS
You need to start this cake the day before. Dip cutters into hot water then dry well before cutting rounds from chocolate.

ben

MOONROCK ICE-CREAM

1 Place biscuits in ziptop plastic bag. Using a rolling pin or meat mallet, gently pound biscuits until broken into large pieces. Grease and line freezerproof bowl with plastic wrap.

2 Place ice-cream in the bowl of an electric mixer with a paddle attachment. Add biscuits and a few drops of black food colouring. Mix until just combined. Spoon mixture into bowl; level top. Freeze overnight.

3 Meanwhile, line oven tray with baking paper. Melt chocolate (page 337); tint grey. Evenly spread chocolate over tray into a thin layer; refrigerate until set. Using cookie cutters, cut various-sized rounds from chocolate.

4 Turn ice-cream onto cake board. Press chocolate rounds onto ice-cream to form moon craters. Sprinkle choc rocks around cake.

EQUIPMENT
- 1 MEDIUM ZIPTOP PLASTIC BAG
- 2.5 LITRE (10-CUP) FREEZERPROOF BOWL
- PLASTIC WRAP
- OVEN TRAY
- 3.5CM (1½-INCH) ROUND CUTTER
- 4.5CM (1¾-INCH) ROUND CUTTER
- 30CM (12-INCH) ROUND CAKE BOARD (PAGE 332)

CAKE
- 200G (6½ OUNCES) CHOCOLATE CREAM-FILLED BISCUITS
- 2 LITRES (8 CUPS) VANILLA ICE-CREAM, SOFTENED
- BLACK FOOD COLOURING SUITABLE FOR CHOCOLATE

DECORATIONS
- 110G (3½ OUNCES) WHITE CHOCOLATE, CHOPPED
- 150G (4½ OUNCES) BLACK AND WHITE CHOC ROCKS

PERIODICALLY, IT'S MY BIRTHDAY

EQUIPMENT

- 35CM X 60CM (14-INCH X 24-INCH) RECTANGULAR CAKE BOARD (PAGE 332)

CAKE

- 2 X 450G (14½-OUNCE) PACKETS DOUBLE UNFILLED SPONGE SLABS
- 1 X 453G (14½-OUNCE) TUB VANILLA FROSTING

DECORATIONS

- 2 X 500G (1-POUND) PACKETS LICORICE ALLSORTS
- YELLOW AND BLACK WRITING ICING

1 Level cake tops (page 333). Secure two of the cakes, long sides touching, on cake board. Spread tops with some of the frosting. Top with remaining cakes. Spread top and sides with frosting.

2 Using a sharp knife; cut licorice allsorts in half (you need 8 yellow, 18 orange, 23 pink and 14 green). Using picture as a guide, position coloured licorice pieces on cake to make periodic table.

3 Write element symbols onto periodic table with yellow writing icing and 'happy birthday' with black writing icing.

LITTLE SHOP OF CUPCAKES

1 Secure one of the cakes to cake board with a little frosting. Spread top with 1/3 cup of the frosting.

2 Cut one-third from the long side of the remaining cake; reserve both cake pieces.

3 Position the larger cake piece on top of the cake on the cake board, so the backs of the cakes are aligned. Spread top with ¼ cup of the frosting.

4 Position the remaining cake piece on top so all cakes are aligned to create steps. Spread top and sides of cake with remaining frosting.

5 Place cupcakes into paper cases; position along the steps.

EQUIPMENT
- 30CM (12-INCH) SQUARE CAKE BOARD (PAGE 332)
- 12 YELLOW MINI PAPER CASES

CAKE
- 1 X 450G (14½-OUNCE) PACKAGED DOUBLE UNFILLED SPONGE SLABS
- 1 X 453G (14½-OUNCE) TUB STRAWBERRY FROSTING

DECORATIONS
- 12 MINI ICED CUPCAKES

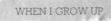

DRUM ROLL, PLEASE

EQUIPMENT

- 1 X 20CM (8-INCH) ROUND CARDBOARD CAKE BOARD
- 2 X 8CM (3¼-INCH) ROUND CARDBOARD CAKE BOARDS
- PAPER PIPING BAG (PAGE 336)
- 50CM (20-INCH) SQUARE CAKE BOARD (PAGE 332)

CAKE

- 1 X 460G (14½-OUNCE) PACKAGED DOUBLE UNFILLED SPONGE CAKE ROUNDS
- 1 QUANTITY WHITE CHOCOLATE GANACHE (PAGE 327)
- 1 X 453G (14½-OUNCE) TUB VANILLA FROSTING
- 6 PACKAGED PAVLOVA NESTS (80G)

DECORATIONS

- 6 X 25G (¾-OUNCE) PACKETS ORANGE SPRINKLES
- 375G (12 OUNCES) WHITE CHOCOLATE MELTS
- 100G (3 OUNCES) WHITE CHOCOLATE MELTS, EXTRA
- 2 CHOCOLATE CREAM WAFER STICKS
- 2 BLUE SPRINKLE LICORICE ALLSORTS
- 14 CHOCOLATE WAFER STICKS
- 16 BLUE SMARTIES

1 Level cake tops (page 333). Secure one of the cakes onto 20cm (8-inch) cake board with a little ganache. Spread top of cake with ½ cup of the ganache; top with remaining cake, cut-side down. Spread sides of cake with frosting. Place sprinkles on a lipped oven tray; roll cake on its side to cover in sprinkles.

2 Secure two of the pavlovas to 8cm (3¼-inch) cake boards with a little ganache; spread tops with ¼ cup of the ganache. Top each with another pavlova; spread tops with ¼ cup of the ganache then top with remaining pavlovas. Spread sides of pavlovas with frosting; carefully roll in sprinkles.

3 Draw a 20cm (8-inch) and two 8cm (3¼-inch) circles on baking paper.

4 Melt chocolate (page 337); spread into each baking-paper circle to form three discs. Stand 10 minutes or until set. Remove baking paper, and secure chocolate discs to top of cake and pavlovas with a little frosting.

5 Melt extra chocolate. Fill paper piping bag with chocolate, snip a small opening in the end; pipe a little chocolate onto one end of each cream wafer stick; attach licorice allsort to make drumsticks, stand until set.

6 Assemble drum kit on 50cm (20-inch) cake board as pictured, secure with a little ganache. Using picture as a guide, decorate sides of large drum cake with wafer sticks and Smarties, securing with a little melted chocolate. Secure drumsticks to cake with a little melted chocolate.

TIP

We used ganache in this recipe to hold the larger drum in place as it sets firmer than frosting.

TIPS

We used a selection of party mix, jubes, Jaffas, jelly beans, Kool Fruits and coloured milk bottles. Edible cake images can be ordered online.

PICTURE PERFECT

1 Preheat oven to 180°C/350°F. Grease cake pan; line base with baking paper.

2 Make cakes according to directions on packets. Spread mixture into pan; bake about 1 hour. Stand cake in pan 5 minutes before turning, top-side up, onto a wire rack to cool.

3 Using a serrated knife, level cake top. Secure cake, cut-side down, on cake board with a little butter cream.

4 Tint butter cream yellow. Spread butter cream all over cake. Centre photograph on cake.

5 Trim snakes; outline photo with red snakes, attach yellow snakes diagonally to corners of cake. Scatter lollies and Smarties all over cake; press gently into butter cream.

EQUIPMENT

- DEEP 23CM (9¼-INCH) SQUARE CAKE PAN
- 35CM (14-INCH) SQUARE CAKE BOARD (PAGE 332)

CAKE

- 2 X 340G (11-OUNCE) PACKETS BUTTER CAKE MIX
- 2 QUANTITIES BUTTER CREAM (PAGE 327)
- YELLOW FOOD COLOURING

DECORATIONS

- 11CM (4½-INCH) SQUARE PHOTOGRAPH, LAMINATED
- 4 EACH RED AND YELLOW JELLY SNAKES
- SELECTION OF LOLLIES (SEE TIPS)
- SMARTIES

VEGETABLE GARDEN

FOR THESE RECIPES YOU WILL NEED 6 MINI UNICED CUPCAKES AND 3 TABLESPOONS READY-MADE VANILLA FROSTING. PLACE CUPCAKES INTO MINI POTS AND SPREAD TOPS WITH FROSTING. QUANTITIES GIVEN ARE ENOUGH TO DECORATE ONE CUPCAKE.

PEAS

Sprinkle 2 teaspoons crushed chocolate biscuits over frosting. Cut 3 spearmint leaves in half horizontally, without cutting all the way through. Push 3 green mini M&M's into each spearmint leaf cavity to make peas in pods, position on cupcake. Tie three knots in 1 green rainbow lace; position on cupcake for pea tendril.

CARROTS

Sprinkle 2 teaspoons crushed chocolate biscuits over frosting. Microwave 3 orange Starburst Chews on High (100%) for 10 seconds or until pliable. Shape into carrots. Using a wooden toothpick, push a hole into the top end of each carrot. Cut a 2cm length of green soft eating licorice into 3 pieces. Snip the ends of each piece for carrot tops; push pieces into holes. Push carrots into cupcake.

PUMPKIN

Sprinkle 2 teaspoons crushed chocolate biscuits over frosting. Tint 2 teaspoons vanilla frosting green; spoon into a small piping bag fitted with a 5mm fluted tube. Using picture as a guide, position 8 small orange jelly beans, upright, side-by-side, in a circle on cupcake, pushing into crushed biscuit. Pipe frosting stalk in centre of circle. Push 2 spearmint leaves into cake.

MUSHROOMS

Sprinkle 2 teaspoons crushed chocolate biscuits over frosting. Using picture as a guide, trim 2 of 3 white milk bottles, so they are three different lengths. Secure a white chocolate Melt to the top of each milk bottle with a little melted chocolate. Position on cupcake, pushing into frosting. Sprinkle with cocoa powder.

Colour me in

Here are some decorating ideas for your crazy cake –photocopy the pattern on page 50 then try different combinations of colours and patterns to make your own.

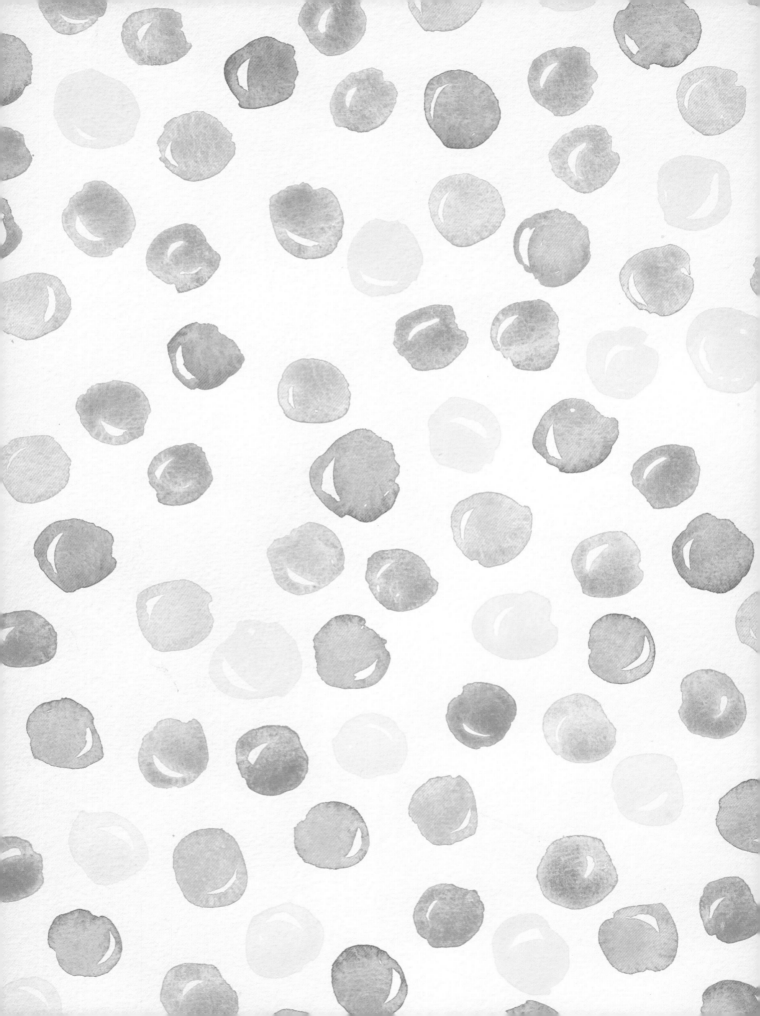

SCIENCE & Adventure

WILDFIRE FLOWER CAKE

EQUIPMENT

- 30CM X 40CM (12-INCH X 16-INCH) RECTANGULAR CAKE BOARD (PAGE 332)

CAKE

- 1 X 450G (14½-OUNCE) PACKAGED DOUBLE UNFILLED SPONGE SLABS
- 1 X 453G (14½-OUNCE) TUB VANILLA FROSTING

DECORATIONS

- 7 RED JELLY SNAKES
- 14 SPEARMINT LEAVES, HALVED
- 7 CREAMY YELLOW JELLY BEANS, HALVED
- 3 RED JELLY BEANS, HALVED
- 4 ORANGE JELLY BEANS, HALVED
- 3 PALE PINK JELLY BEANS, HALVED
- 1 BRIGHT YELLOW JELLY BEAN, HALVED
- 3 RED SQUARE JUBES, HALVED
- 2 YELLOW SQUARE JUBES, HALVED
- 4 EACH ORANGE AND RED OVAL JUBES, HALVED
- 4 PALE PINK SQUARE JUBES, HALVED
- 2 PINK OVAL JUBES, HALVED
- 3 PURPLE RECTANGLE JUBES, HALVED
- 5 EACH YELLOW AND ORANGE RECTANGLE JUBES, HALVED
- 9 RED RECTANGLE JUBES, HALVED
- 1 ORANGE OVAL JUBE
- 2 TEASPOONS RAINBOW NERDS
- 1 GREEN JELLY SNAKE, SLICED THINLY

1 Secure cakes, side-by-side, to cake board with a little frosting; spread top and sides with frosting.

2 Tie red snakes into knots; trim tails, discard tails. Using picture as a guide, decorate cake top with knotted snake heads, spearmint leaves, jelly beans, jubes and nerds to make flower patterns on cake. Use thinly sliced green snake to make stems and tendrils.

TIPS If using butter cream instead of frosting, you will need one quantity of butter cream (page 327). We used a variety of jubes to get different shapes.

AROUND THE OLD CAMPFIRE

1 Preheat oven to 150°C/300°F. Line oven tray with baking paper.

2 Split each cake in half. Secure one cake round to cake board with a little frosting; spread 1/3 cup of the frosting over cake, top with another cake round. Repeat with 1/3 cup of the frosting and one more cake round. (Reserve remaining cake round for another use – you could use it to make cake pops). Spread remaining frosting over sides and top of cake.

3 Place lollipops in plastic sandwich bag; using a rolling pin or meat mallet, gently smash lollipops until broken into pieces; discard sticks. Place lollipop pieces onto oven tray; place in oven for 5 minutes or until melted and edges are starting to brown. Cool on tray; set aside until needed.

4 Carefully cut Flakes in half crossways. Break melted lollipops into large shards. Using picture as a guide, arrange shards on cake to form fire; arrange Flakes around toffee for logs. Position chocolate fingers around side of cake.

TIPS If using butter cream instead of chocolate frosting, you will need two quantities of chocolate butter cream (page 327). The melted lollipops are best made on day of serving as humidity may cause them to dissolve. Use a variety of chocolate bars – such as Flakes, Violet Crumbles or Tim Tam biscuits – for campfire logs.

EQUIPMENT

- OVEN TRAY
- 30CM (12-INCH) ROUND CAKE BOARD (PAGE 332)
- PLASTIC SANDWICH BAG

CAKE

- 2 X 600G (1¼-POUND) PACKETS ROUND CHOCOLATE MUD CAKES
- 1½ X 453G (14½-OUNCE) TUBS DARK CHOCOLATE FROSTING

DECORATIONS

- 5 ORANGE LOLLIPOPS
- 5 YELLOW LOLLIPOPS
- 5 RED LOLLIPOPS
- 4 X 30G (1-OUNCE) BARS CHOCOLATE FLAKES
- 2 X 125G (4-OUNCE) PACKETS CHOCOLATE FINGER BISCUITS

BUTTERFLY DISPLAY CASE

EQUIPMENT

- 30CM (12-INCH) SQUARE CAKE BOARD (PAGE 332)
- PAPER PIPING BAG (PAGE 336)

CAKE

- ½ X 450G (14½-OUNCE) PACKAGED DOUBLE UNFILLED SPONGE SLABS
- ½ CUP (170G) CREAM CHEESE FROSTING
- ½ CUP (170G) DARK CHOCOLATE FROSTING

DECORATIONS

- ⅓ CUP (50G) MILK CHOCOLATE MELTS
- 5 X 30G (1-OUNCE) BARS CHOCOLATE FLAKES
- 8 CHOCOLATE FINGER BISCUITS
- 1 RAINBOW BERRY ROLL-UP
- 1 RAINBOW ROLL-UP
- 2 RED LICORICE TUBES

1 Level cake top (page 333). Secure cake, cut-side down, on cake board with a little cream cheese frosting. Spread chocolate frosting over sides of cake. Spread cream cheese frosting over top of cake.

2 Melt chocolate (page 337). Using picture as a guide, cut and position Flakes for frame. Place melted chocolate into a piping bag; snip end to make a small opening. Pipe chocolate onto corners of frame to secure Flakes together. Secure biscuits on each corner of frame with a little melted chocolate.

3 Using kitchen scissors, cut butterfly shapes from roll-ups. Trim excess to make antennae and wing decorations.

4 Using picture as a guide, secure butterflies to cake with a little melted chocolate; attach licorice in middle of wings for bodies, then attach antennae and wing decorations.

TIP If using butter cream instead of cream cheese frosting, you will need to make one quantity of butter cream (page 327). Tint half the mixture light yellow; add 1½ tablespoons cocoa powder to remaining mixture for chocolate butter cream.

SCIENCE EXPERIMENT SPILL

1 Level the cake tops (page 333). Secure one cake, cut-side down, on cake board. Spread top with 1/3 cup of the chocolate frosting; top with remaining cake. Spread chocolate frosting over top and side of cake.

2 Brush wafers with orange colouring mixed with a little water to make wire fence. Position wafers around side of cake. Wrap tape around cake, secure with a little frosting.

3 Trim tops of ice-cream cones from bases with a serrated knife. Paint two tops with yellow colouring mixed with a little water; stand 10 minutes or until dry. Repeat with green colouring. Paint two bases with red colouring mixed with a little water; stand 10 minutes or until dry. Discard remaining two bases.

Stack ice-cream cones, top ends together, to form barrels; secure with a little frosting.

4 Divide vanilla frosting between three microwave safe bowls. Tint yellow, green and red. Microwave frosting on medium (50%) for 20 seconds or until melted.

5 Using picture as a guide, position barrels on cake; fill barrels with frosting; decorate with nerds and choc chips. Pour remaining warmed frosting on top of cake, allowing it to spill over sides.

TIP The biohazard tape was ordered online. Printing the words 'biohazard' onto yellow tape with a permanent marker adds a visual effect which is just as good, and less expensive.

EQUIPMENT
- 30CM (12-INCH) ROUND CAKE BOARD (PAGE 332)
- SMALL NEW ARTISTS' PAINT BRUSH

CAKE
- 2 X 20CM (8-INCH) ROUND CHOCOLATE CAKES
- 1 X 453G (14½-OUNCE) TUB DARK CHOCOLATE FROSTING
- ORANGE, YELLOW, GREEN AND RED FOOD COLOURING
- ½ X 453G (14½-OUNCE) TUB VANILLA FROSTING

DECORATIONS
- ½ X 80G (2½-OUNCE) PACKET WAFER BISCUITS
- 65CM (26-INCH) TAPE OR RIBBON (SEE TIP)
- 4 FLAT-BASED ICE-CREAM CONES
- 1 TEASPOON EACH GREEN AND YELLOW NERDS
- 1 TEASPOON RED RAINBOW CHOC CHIPS

ROBBIE 2.0

EQUIPMENT

- 30CM X 40CM (12-INCH X 16-INCH) RECTANGULAR CAKE BOARD (PAGE 332)
- 2 BAMBOO SKEWERS

CAKE

- 2 X 450G (14½-OUNCE) PACKAGED DOUBLE UNFILLED SPONGE SLABS
- 2 QUANTITIES BUTTER CREAM (PAGE 327)
- BLUE AND RED FOOD COLOURING

DECORATIONS

- 12 VANILLA MACAROONS
- 2 BLUE SOUR TUBES, HALVED
- 6 BLUE SPRINKLE LICORICE ALLSORTS
- 5 EACH OF YELLOW AND RED FRUIT ROLLS
- 1 RED LICORICE TUBE
- 3 X 1 METRE (40-INCH) PIECE BLACK LICORICE STRAPS
- 6 LICORICE ALLSORTS, BLUE PART ONLY
- 6 HEART-SHAPED JUBES
- 4 GREEN FRUIT ROLLS
- 4 WHITE CHOCOLATE MELTS
- ⅓ X 180G (5½-OUNCE) BLOCK WHITE CHOCOLATE
- 1 EACH OF BLUE, RED, YELLOW AND GREEN M&M'S
- 4 EACH OF YELLOW, ORANGE AND RED MINI M&M'S

1 Secure two of the cakes onto cake board with a little butter cream. Using a serrated knife, cut one of the remaining cakes into a 12cm (4¾-inch) square. Cut remaining cake into a 4cm x 14cm (1½-inch x 5½-inch) rectangle. Using picture as a guide, secure cakes to cake board with a little butter cream.

2 Tint two-thirds of the butter cream blue. Tint remaining butter cream red.

3 Using picture as a guide, spread blue butter cream over top and sides of robot body. Spread red butter cream over top and sides of head. Position macaroons as robots arms; secure with a little butter cream.

4 Push two of the sour tube halves onto skewers; place a blue allsort on one end and a red and yellow fruit roll on the other end. Push into cake as antennae. Secure remaining sour tubes to make mouth.

5 Cut two red fruit rolls into claws, as pictured; secure to the end of arms.

6 Trim licorice tube into an arrow shape. Using picture as a guide, decorate robot's head and body with remaining lollies; secure decorations with a little butter cream.

TIPS Macaroons are available from speciality bakery shops and select supermarkets. If you can't find them, any small round filled biscuit will do. Try mini Oreos or Wagon Wheels, or Monte Carlos. Colour the butter cream and decorate the robot using any colours you like. Fruit Mentos and Smarties come in pastel colours, if you prefer these shades to the bolder ones used here. Be sure to remove the skewers from the cake before cutting and serving.

VOLCANO VOMITUS

1 Preheat oven to 150°C/300°F. Line oven tray with baking paper.

2 Secure one cake to cake board with a little frosting. Spread cake top with 1/3 cup of the chocolate frosting; top with remaining cake. Using a small serrated knife, trim cake into a volcano shape. Secure doughnut to top of cake with a little frosting. Spread remaining chocolate frosting over top and sides of cake.

3 Place boiled lollies into sandwich bag and gently smash with a rolling pin or meat mallet until broken into small pieces. Place pieces onto oven tray; place in oven for 10 minutes or until lollies have melted. Use the back of a metal spoon to thin out edges. Cool toffee on tray.

4 Discard chocolate coating from honeycomb. Roughly chop honeycomb.

5 Tint coconut yellow (page 336). Using picture as a guide, position coconut, honeycomb and nerds around base and sides of volcano. Tint vanilla frosting orange in a small microwave safe bowl. Microwave frosting on medium (50%) for 20 seconds or until melted.

6 Pour orange frosting around top and down sides of volcano. Break cooled toffee into pieces; position in top of volcano as fire.

TIPS Toffee is best made on the day of serving. You could use red and yellow lollipops to make the toffee following step 3. You need to buy a packet of rainbow nerds as these contain orange nerds.

EQUIPMENT

- OVEN TRAY
- 30CM (12-INCH) ROUND CAKE BOARD (PAGE 332)
- SANDWICH BAG

CAKE

- 1 X 460G (14½-OUNCE) PACKAGED DOUBLE UNFILLED SPONGE CAKE ROUNDS
- 1 X 453G (14½-OUNCE) TUB DARK CHOCOLATE FROSTING
- 1 CINNAMON DOUGHNUT
- 1 X 453G (14½-OUNCE) TUB VANILLA FROSTING
- YELLOW AND ORANGE FOOD COLOURING

DECORATIONS

- 50G (1½ OUNCES) ORANGE BOILED LOLLIES OR BARLEY SUGAR
- 50G (1½ OUNCES) RED BOILED LOLLIES
- 50G (1½ OUNCES) YELLOW BOILED LOLLIES
- 2 X 50G (1½-OUNCE) BARS CHOCOLATE-COATED HONEYCOMB OR PLAIN HONEYCOMB
- 1 CUP (75G) MOIST COCONUT FLAKES
- ¼ CUP (65G) ORANGE NERDS (SEE TIPS)

BUG CATCHER

EQUIPMENT

- 20CM X 30CM (8-INCH X 12-INCH) RECTANGULAR CAKE BOARD (PAGE 332)

CAKE

- 1 X 450G (14½-OUNCE) PACKAGED DOUBLE UNFILLED SPONGE SLABS
- 1 X 453G (14½-OUNCE) TUB VANILLA FROSTING

DECORATIONS

- ¼ CUP (45G) MILK CHOCOLATE BITS
- ¼ CUP (45G) DARK CHOCOLATE BITS
- 26 SPEARMINT LEAVES, HALVED
- 9 CHOCOLATE LADYBIRDS

1 Position one cake lengthways on cake board; secure with a little frosting. Secure remaining cake, crossways, touching the top edge of the first cake with a little frosting.

2 Using a small serrated knife, cut the upper cake to create a funnel shape. Spread frosting over top and sides of cakes.

3 Decorate the bottom edge of the cake with combined chocolate bits for 'dirt'. Using picture as a guide, decorate cake with spearmint leaves and ladybirds.

TIPS We used Tic Tacs to make the ladybird 'trail'. Use as many ladybirds as you like to decorate the cake board. Use any critter lollies you can find, sour worms work well, or even use plastic spiders, if you like. If using non-edible decorations, make sure they are removed before serving. If using butter cream instead of vanilla frosting, you will need one quantity of butter cream (page 327).

A BLIZZARD OF SNOWMEN

1 Place sifted sugar on a large plate. Roll jam doughnuts in sugar to coat. Repeat with cinnamon doughnuts and mini doughnuts.

2 Secure jam doughnuts on serving plates with a little frosting. Top with cinnamon doughnuts and mini doughnuts to create snowmen, securing each doughnut with a little frosting.

3 Insert sticks into cinnamon doughnuts to form arms. Secure mini M&M's with a little frosting to form eyes. Trim jelly babies into wedges to create carrot noses. Insert into centre of mini doughnut.

TIPS Use a mixture of jam and cinnamon doughnuts, mini jam doughnuts and doughnut holes, if you like. Be sure to remove the sticks from the snowmen before serving.

EQUIPMENT

- 6 SERVING PLATES, OR A LARGE SERVING TRAY

CAKE

- ½ CUP (80G) ICING (CONFECTIONERS') SUGAR
- 6 JAM DOUGHNUTS
- 6 CINNAMON DOUGHNUTS
- 6 MINI CINNAMON DOUGHNUTS
- ½ CUP (170G) VANILLA FROSTING

DECORATIONS

- 12 SMALL CLEAN STICKS, OR BROWN CHENILLE STICKS (PIPE CLEANERS)
- 12 BROWN MINI M&M'S
- 6 ORANGE JELLY BABIES

MAGNOSCOPIC WORMS

EQUIPMENT

- 40CM (16-INCH) ROUND CAKE BOARD (PAGE 332)

CAKE

- 1 X 85G (3-OUNCE) PACKET CREATE-A-JELLY CRYSTALS
- 1 TEASPOON ORANGE ESSENCE
- 1 X 600G (1¼-POUND) PACKET WHITE CHOCOLATE MUD CAKE
- 2 CHOCOLATE ROLLETTES
- 1 QUANTITY BUTTER CREAM (PAGE 327)
- 2 TABLESPOONS COCOA POWDER

DECORATIONS

- 3 KILLER PYTHONS
- 2 YELLOW JELLY SNAKES
- 1 PURPLE JELLY SNAKE

1 Make jelly following packet directions; stir in essence. Pour into a shallow dish; refrigerate 30 minutes or until jelly is the consistency of unbeaten egg whites.

2 Meanwhile, using a small serrated knife and a tablespoon, scoop out a recess in centre of cake about 3cm (1¼-inch) deep, leaving a 2.5cm (1-inch) border around edge. Secure cake on cake board with a little butter cream.

3 Reserve one-third of the butter cream. Stir cocoa powder into remaining butter cream. Spread inside of recess with reserved plain butter cream.

4 Attach rollettes to one end of cake with a little butter cream to make a magnifying glass handle; spread chocolate butter cream over handle, and top and sides of cake.

5 Cut pythons in half, discard tail end. Position pythons in recess of cake. Spoon enough jelly over pythons to cover them and come up to the rim of the cake. Refrigerate cake until jelly is set.

6 Cut heads from snakes; discard. Attach snakes to outside of cake to match pythons, as pictured, to give the illusion of 'worm' tails.

TIPS Create-a-jelly crystals give a clear jelly, which can be coloured however you like. It is available from major supermarkets. We used a heavier-crumbed mud cake, as it is more solid and less likely to allow the jelly to leak. We used butter cream instead of ready-made frosting as it is firmer and less likely to break down into the jelly.

TIP
Board shorts can be completed a day before the party. Store in an airtight container at a cool room temperature.

BEACH BOARDIES

1 Preheat oven to 180°C/350°F. Grease baking dish; line base and sides with baking paper, extending paper 5cm (2-inch) above sides.

2 Make cakes according to directions on packets. Spread mixture into dish; bake about 1 hour. Stand cake in dish 10 minutes before turning, top-side up, onto a wire rack to cool.

3 Using a serrated knife, level cake top; turn cake cut-side down. Using picture as a guide, cut out boardies shape from cake using ruler to cut the straight edges. Secure cake, cut-side down, on cake board.

4 Tint butter cream turquoise using both colourings; spread all over cake.

5 Knead ready-made icing on a surface dusted with a little sifted icing sugar until icing loses its stickiness. Roll out on a surface dusted with a little icing sugar until 3mm (⅛-inch) thick. Cut a 3cm (1¼-inch) waistband from icing. Position waistband on cake. Attach cord around cake; tie with a bow.

6 Cut strawberry off strawberries & cream; using picture as a guide, pinch end to make a petal. Position jubes and Smarties to complete flowers.

EQUIPMENT
- 26CM X 35CM (10½-INCH X 14-INCH) BAKING DISH
- RULER
- 30CM X 40CM (12-INCH X 16-INCH) RECTANGULAR CAKE BOARD (PAGE 332)

CAKE
- 4 X 340G (11-OUNCE) PACKETS BUTTER CAKE MIX
- 2 QUANTITIES BUTTER CREAM (PAGE 327)
- TURQUOISE AND BLUE FOOD COLOURING

DECORATIONS
- 90G (3 QUNCES) READY-MADE WHITE ICING (PAGE 327)
- PURE ICING (CONFECTIONERS') SUGAR, FOR DUSTING
- 45CM (18-INCH) LENGTH POLYESTER CORD
- 30 STRAWBERRIES & CREAM LOLLLIES
- 10 OVAL GREEN JUBES, HALVED
- 6 YELLOW SMARTIES

FROGS IN A POND

EQUIPMENT

- 26CM X 35CM (10½-INCH X 14-INCH) BAKING DISH
- 20CM X 30CM (8-INCH X 12-INCH) SHALLOW PAN
- 25CM X 30CM (10-INCH X 12-INCH) RECTANGULAR CAKE BOARD (PAGE 332)

CAKE

- 4 X 340G (11-OUNCE) PACKETS BUTTER CAKE MIX
- 2 X 85G (3-OUNCE) PACKETS CREATE-A-JELLY CRYSTALS
- BLUE AND KELLY GREEN FOOD COLOURING
- 1 QUANTITY BUTTER CREAM (PAGE 327)

DECORATIONS

- 8 RED FROGS
- 2 LIME MILK BOTTLES
- 8 READY-MADE SUGAR FLOWERS
- 2 FLAG CAKE TOPPERS
- 1 EACH RED AND ORANGE JUBES
- 2 BROWN PAPER TREES
- BIRTHDAY CANDLES

1 Preheat oven to 180°C/350°F. Grease baking dish; line base and sides with baking paper, extending paper 5cm (2-inch) above sides.

2 Make cakes according to directions on packets. Spread mixture into baking dish; bake about 1 hour. Stand cake in dish 10 minutes before turning, top-side up, onto a wire rack to cool.

3 Make jelly following packet directions; tint light blue with colouring. Pour into shallow pan. Refrigerate for 1 hour or until jelly is the consistency of unbeaten egg whites.

4 Meanwhile, using a long serrated knife, level cake top. Using picture as a guide, cut out pond shape. Using a small serrated knife and a tablespoon, scoop out a recess in centre of cake, about 4cm (1½-inch) deep, leaving a 2cm (¾-inch) border around edges of pond. Secure cake on cake board with a little butter cream.

5 Reserve ¼ cup of the butter cream. Tint remaining butter cream green; spread over sides and top edge of cake. Spread reserved plain butter cream over recess of cake. When jelly is ready, pour into recess in cake; refrigerate until jelly is set.

6 Using picture as a guide, decorate cake. Place frogs in and around jelly. To make lily pads, slice milk bottles into thin rounds; flatten slightly. Using a small sharp knife, cut a 'V' shape into each slice. Position lily pads and sugar flowers on set jelly (see tips).

7 Trim ends of cake toppers, push into jubes to make boats; position on jelly. Decorate border with trees and candles.

TIPS

Create-a-jelly crystals give a clear jelly, which can be coloured however you like. It is available from major supermarkets. Decorate the jelly just before serving.

ADDY THE ALIEN

1 Preheat oven to 180°C/350°F. Grease cake pans; line bases with baking paper.

2 Make cakes according to directions on packets. Divide mixture between pans so both mixtures are the same depth. Bake round cake about 35 minutes; bake oval cake about 40 minutes. Stand cakes in pans 5 minutes before turning, top-side up, onto wire racks to cool.

3 Using a serrated knife, level cake tops so they are the same height. Secure cakes, cut-side down, to cake board with a little butter cream.

4 Tint butter cream pale green; spread over cakes.

5 Position peaches & cream for eyes, and lip for mouth. Position nerds on cheeks and forehead; position lollipops on head for antennae.

6 Skewer each banana with a toothpick; position on sides of head. Position Kool Fruits, Gobstoppers and Smarties on body of alien.

TIPS Lips, peaches & cream and bananas can be found in packets of party mix. Be sure to remove the toothpicks from the cake before cutting and serving. Use all the colours of Kool Fruits and make Addy a multi-coloured alien, if you like.

EQUIPMENT

- **DEEP 20CM (8-INCH) ROUND CAKE PAN**
- **DEEP 18CM (7¼-INCH) OVAL CAKE PAN**
- **30CM X 46CM (12-INCH X 18½-INCH) RECTANGULAR CAKE BOARD (PAGE 332)**

CAKE

- **2 X 340G (11-OUNCE) PACKETS BUTTER CAKE MIX**
- **2 QUANTITIES BUTTER CREAM (PAGE 327)**
- **GREEN FOOD COLOURING**

DECORATIONS

- **2 PEACHES & CREAM LOLLIES**
- **1 JELLY LIP**
- **29 ORANGE NERDS**
- **2 PINK NERDS**
- **2 GREEN LOLLIPOPS**
- **4 YELLOW BANANA LOLLIES**
- **4 WOODEN TOOTHPICKS**
- **15 EACH ORANGE AND YELLOW KOOL FRUITS**
- **20 EACH GREEN AND YELLOW GOBSTOPPERS**
- **14 GREEN SMARTIES**

NIGHT LIFE

IN THE FOREST

EQUIPMENT

- 30CM (12-INCH) ROUND CAKE BOARD (PAGE 332)
- 1 MEDIUM ZIPTOP PLASTIC BAG
- DISPOSABLE PLASTIC PIPING BAG

CAKE

- 2 X 600G (1¼-POUND) PACKETS ROUND CHOCOLATE CAKE
- 1 X 453G (14½-OUNCE) TUB DARK CHOCOLATE FROSTING

DECORATIONS

- 1 CUP (80G) DESICCATED COCONUT
- GREEN FOOD COLOURING
- 8 GREEN LOLLIPOPS
- 200G (6½ OUNCES) DARK CHOCOLATE MELTS
- 2 RAINBOW ROLL-UPS
- 1 THIN WAFER STICK, HALVED CROSSWAYS
- 1 X 30G (1-OUNCE) BAR CHOCOLATE FLAKE
- WHITE CHOCOLATE ROCKS
- 2 PRETZEL STICKS
- 2 MINI MARSHMALLOWS, HALVED
- MINIATURE BUNTING
- 2 PAPER DRINKING STRAWS

1 Level cake tops (page 333). Secure one cake, cut-side down, on cake board. Spread cake top with 1/3 cup of the chocolate frosting; top with remaining cake. Spread chocolate frosting over top and side of cake. Tint coconut green (page 336). Sprinkle coconut over top of cake.

2 Place lollipops into ziptop bag. Use a rolling pin to pound into small pieces; discard sticks.

3 Melt chocolate (page 337). Fill piping bag with melted chocolate. Pipe two trees onto baking paper (see tips). Before chocolate sets, sprinkle branches with crushed lollipops and lightly score down the centre of one tree. Stand 10 minutes or until set.

4 Remove trees from baking paper. Using a sharp knife, cut down the centre of scored tree to cut in half.

Using a little melted chocolate, secure the straight sides of the cut tree to the uncut tree on either side; stand upright on baking paper until set.

5 Fold one of the roll-ups in half to form a tent; secure a wafer at each end of the roll-up with a little chocolate. Push into cake to secure.

6 Using picture as a guide, position tree on cake, gently pushing into frosting.

7 Break Flake into pieces and position on cake for campfire logs. Cut remaining roll-up into random pieces and position on logs for fire. Surround campfire with choc rocks. Break pretzels in half; push a marshmallow onto each pretzel and place around fire.

8 Secure bunting to drinking straws; push straws into cake, as pictured.

TIP

Trace two tree shapes onto baking paper. Turn the paper over and pipe within the outline of the tree. Once set, one tree is secured to the other for a 3D effect.

TIP

You can make the frozen lake out of ready-made white icing, if you like.

SKATING
ON THIN ICE

1 Make jelly following packet directions; tint with a little blue colouring. Place take-away container lid on a small tray; fill with about ¼ cup (60ml) of the jelly. Refrigerate 1 hour or until set.

2 Melt te white chocolate (page 337). Place ice-cream cones on an oven tray lined with baking paper; drizzle cones with some of the melted chocolate to completely cover, sprinkle with coconut. Stand 10 minutes or until chocolate sets.

3 To make snowmen, secure 2 Raffaello chocolates together with a little melted chocolate. Secure trimmed licorice strap for eyes and trimmed orange licorice allsort for nose with a little melted chocolate. Cut sour strap lengthways into coloured sections; use blue and green strips from sour strap to make scarves, wrap around snowmen.

4 Trim one cake layer into a 12cm (4¾-inch) round; place muffin on top. Position a large marshmallow next to muffin for entrance of igloo. Secure cake rounds, side by side, on cake board with a little frosting. Using picture as a guide, use a small sharp knife to carefully cut an 11cm (4½-inch) round with a 1cm (½-inch) deep cavity into larger cake round; scoop out cake from cavity with a teaspoon. Spread frosting all over cake.

5 Using picture as a guide, trim remaining licorice strap for igloo door. Position marshmallows on muffin for igloo. Position cones and snowmen on cake. Just before serving, carefully push take-away container lid into cavity. Sprinkle cake with extra coconut.

EQUIPMENT
- 11CM (4½-INCH) ROUND PLASTIC TAKE-AWAY CONTAINER LID
- 30CM X 45CM (12-INCH X 18-INCH) RECTANGULAR CAKE BOARD (PAGE 332)

CAKE
- 1 X 460G (1¼-POUND) PACKET DOUBLE UNFILLED SPONGE CAKE ROUNDS
- 1 X MINI CHOCOLATE-CHIP MUFFIN
- 1 X 453G (14½-OUNCE) TUB VANILLA FROSTING

DECORATIONS
- 1 X 85G (3-OUNCE) PACKET CREATE-A-JELLY CRYSTALS
- BLUE FOOD COLOURING
- 100G (3 OUNCES) WHITE CHOCOLATE MELTS
- 1 ICE-CREAM CONE
- 1 MINI ICE-CREAM CONE
- 1 CUP (80G) DESICCATED COCONUT
- 4 RAFFAELLO CHOCOLATES
- 2CM (¾-INCH) PIECE BLACK LICORICE STRAP
- 1 LICORICE ALLSORT, ORANGE LAYER ONLY
- 1 RAINBOW SOUR STRAP
- 10 WHITE MARSHMALLOWS
- 16 WHITE MINI MARSHMALLOWS
- ½ CUP (40G) DESICCATED COCONUT, EXTRA

CONICAL FLASK
CONUNDRUM

EQUIPMENT

- 30CM (12-INCH) ROUND CAKE BOARD (PAGE 332)

CAKE

- 1½ X 453G (14½-OUNCE) TUBS VANILLA FROSTING
- BLACK, GREEN, YELLOW AND BLUE FOOD COLOURING GEL
- 2 X 600G (1¼-POUND) PACKETS ROUND CHOCOLATE CAKES

DECORATIONS

- 200G (6½ OUNCE) WHITE CHOCOLATE MELTS
- 2 LARGE WAFFLE ICE-CREAM CONES
- 1 MINI WAFFLE CONE
- BLACK WRITING GEL
- GREEN, YELLOW AND BLUE NERDS

1 Melt chocolate (page 337). Place cones on an oven tray lined with baking paper. Drizzle cones with melted chocolate to completely cover. Stand 10 minutes or until chocolate sets. Using picture as a guide, mark black lines onto cones with writing gel.

2 Reserve ¾ cup of the frosting. Using black colouring, tint remaining frosting grey. Level top of cakes (page 333). Secure one cake onto cake board with a little frosting. Spread a little frosting over cake then top with remaining cake. Cover top and sides of cake with remaining grey frosting.

3 Divide reserved frosting into three small bowls. Tint frostings green, yellow and blue. Spread base of each cone in one of the coloured frostings then sprinkle with matching nerds. Using picture as a guide, position cones on cake.

TIPS Fill the cones with lollies so the children get a surprise when they lift the cones. You could make lolly filled volcanoes by enclosing the base of the cone with a disc of chocolate. This could make for great lolly bags.

GREAT BALL OF FIRE

1 Melt chocolate (page 337); tint orange with colouring. Dip ice-cream cones, one at a time, into chocolate to coat, drain off excess; cover with sprinkles. Stand on a baking-paper-lined tray; refrigerate until set.

2 Tint frosting the same orange as chocolate cones.

3 Trim icing from top of cakes. Secure one of the cakes to cake board with a little frosting; spread cake with ¼ cup of the frosting, top with remaining cake. Trim edges to make a dome shape. Spread orange frosting all over cake.

4 Fill ice-cream cones with mixed lollies; push firmly all around outside of cake. Sprinkle with nerds.

TIP Mix yellow and red food colouring to make orange if you can't find an orange colour. A powder or gel-based colour is best to add to chocolate. A liquid colour will seize the chocolate, turning it grainy and unusable.

EQUIPMENT
- 50CM (20-INCH) ROUND CAKE BOARD (PAGE 332)

CAKE
- ORANGE FOOD COLOURING
- 2 X 600G (1¼-POUND) PACKETS WHITE MUD CAKES
- 1 X 453G (14½-OUNCE) TUB VANILLA FROSTING

DECORATIONS
- 375G (12 OUNCES) WHITE CHOCOLATE MELTS
- 20 MINI WAFFLE ICE-CREAM CONES
- 6 X 25G (¾-OUNCE) PACKETS ORANGE SPRINKLES
- MIXED LOLLIES, TO FILL ICE-CREAM CONES
- 200G (½ CUP) MIXED ORANGE AND YELLOW NERDS

FESTERING PETRI DISHES!

EQUIPMENT

- 35CM X 60CM (14-INCH X 24-INCH) RECTANGULAR CAKE BOARD (PAGE 332)

CAKE

- 1 X 85G (3-OUNCE) PACKET MANGO JELLY CRYSTALS
- 3 X 600G (1¼-POUND) PACKETS WHITE MUD CAKES
- 2 QUANTITIES BUTTER CREAM (PAGE 327)

DECORATIONS

- 4 SOUR WORMS
- 3 BLUE SPRINKLE LICORICE ALLSORTS
- 11 WHITE TIC TACS
- 1 BLUE BOOTLACE
- 1 GREEN BOOTLACE

1 Make jelly following packet directions. Pour jelly into a shallow dish; refrigerate 30 minutes or until jelly is the consistency of unbeaten egg white.

2 Trim icing from cakes. Use a small sharp knife and a tablespoon to scoop out a recess in centre of each cake, about 2cm (¾-inch) deep, leaving a 2cm (¾-inch) border around edges. Secure cakes on cake board with a little butter cream. Spread butter cream all over cakes.

3 Pour jelly into cakes. Push sour worms into jelly in one of the cakes. Refrigerate all cakes until jelly is set.

4 Position blue licorice allsorts and Tic Tacs on another cake to resemble microbes.

5 For remaining cake, cut blue bootlace into small pieces, sprinkle on top of jelly. Cut green bootlace in half; tie a knot in each half and place on top of the jelly for a virus.

TIPS We used a heavier-crumbed mud cake as it is more solid and less likely to allow the jelly to leak. Butter cream is firmer than ready-made icing and is less likely to break down into the jelly.

Do you want to go on an adventure? Let's get outdoors and make a cubby. Let's climb trees and watch birds and learn all about bugs, insects and creepy crawlies.

TIPS

This recipe makes
15 eyeballs and
3 litres of jelly.
Eyeballs can be made
2 days ahead. Store
at room temperature.
Assemble eyeballs in
jars on day of serving.

I'M WATCHING YOU!

1 Process cake into crumbs. Combine crumbs and frosting in a large bowl; roll 2 teaspoonfuls of the mixture into balls. Place on an oven tray, loosely cover with plastic wrap. Refrigerate 2 hours or until firm.

2 Knead ready-made icing on a surface dusted with icing sugar until icing loses its stickiness. Roll icing on a surface lightly dusted with icing sugar until 3mm (⅛-inch) thick. Brush cake balls with jam. Using cutter, cut rounds from icing; wrap each round around a cake ball, pinching ends to seal. Stand, uncovered, for 4 hours for icing to dry.

3 Slice strawberries into 2cm (¾-inch) rounds, about 3mm (⅛-inch) thick. Using a sharp knife, discard centre of strawberry pieces; place strawberries on paper towel to remove excess moisture. Place a piece of licorice in centre of each strawberry, trimming if necessary. Repeat with kiwifruit.

4 Melt chocolate (page 337). Secure strawberry and kiwifruit to eyeballs with a little melted chocolate. Using picture as a guide, draw lines on eyeballs with black pen.

5 Meanwhile, make jelly following packet directions; tint pale blue. Add a few drops of lime essence. Divide jelly between jars. Refrigerate 1½ hours or until partially set.

6 Push eyeballs into partially set jelly. Refrigerate until jelly is completely set.

EQUIPMENT

- 10CM (4-INCH) ROUND CUTTER
- 5 X 350ML (¾ PINT) CLEAR JARS

CAKE

- 1 X 460G (14½-OUNCE) PACKET DOUBLE UNFILLED SPONGE CAKE ROUNDS
- ½ CUP (150G) READY-MADE VANILLA FROSTING
- 3 X 85G (3-OUNCE) PACKETS CREATE-A-JELLY CRYSTALS
- BLUE FOOD COLOURING
- LIME ESSENCE

DECORATIONS

- 600G (1¼ POUNDS) READY-MADE WHITE ICING
- PURE ICING (CONFECTIONERS') SUGAR, FOR DUSTING
- APRICOT JAM, WARMED
- 250G FRESH STRAWBERRIES
- 3 SOFT EATING LICORICE, SLICED THINLY
- 2 KIWIFRUIT
- 30G (1 OUNCE) WHITE CHOCOLATE MELTS
- NON-TOXIC EDIBLE BLACK PEN

THE START OF THE
BIGBANG

1 Cut 3 x 10.5cm, 2 x 9cm and 3 x 8cm rounds from cakes using cutters. Use 3.5cm cutter to cut centres from two of the 8cm rounds and one of the 9cm rounds. Use 5.5cm cutter to cut centres from two of the 10.5cm rounds. Split one of each centre through the middle to make two rounds.

2 Stack the same-sized rounds on top of each other, securing with a little frosting. Secure to cake board with a little frosting. Pour popping toppings into centre of each cake. Top each cake with one of the cut-out rounds to fill each cake hole. Discard remaining cake pieces. Secure all three stacks with skewers, trimming skewers as required.

3 Divide frosting into three bowls. Tint red, yellow and blue. Using picture as a guide, spread frostings over cakes.

4 Secure M&M's around cakes. Using scissors, cut licorice into three 4cm (1½-inch) thin strips. Position on top of cakes as wicks.

TIPS Popping topping is available from the baking aisle of supermarkets, or buy individual packets of popping candy from the confectionery aisle. Remove skewers before serving cakes.

EQUIPMENT
- 3.5CM, 5.5CM, 8CM, 9CM AND 10.5CM (1½-, 2¼-, 3¼-, 3¾- AND 4¼-INCH) ROUND CUTTERS
- 30CM X 40XM (12-INCH X 16-INCH) RECTANGULAR CAKE BOARD (PAGE 332)
- WOODEN SKEWERS

CAKE
- 2 X 460G (14½-OUNCE) PACKETS DOUBLE UNFILLED SPONGE CAKE SLABS

- 2 X 453G (14½-OUNCE) TUBS VANILLA FROSTING
- RED, YELLOW AND BLUE GEL FOOD COLOURING

DECORATIONS
- 150G (4½-OUNCE) PACKET POPPING TOPPINGS
- 76 YELLOW MINI M&M'S
- 56 ORANGE MINI M&M'S
- 68 BLUE MINI M&M'S
- 12CM (4¾-INCH) BLACK LICORICE STRAP

BUSY WORKING AT THE ANT FARM

1 Bring cream just to the boil in a small saucepan; remove from heat. Pour cream over chocolate in a small heatproof bowl; stir until smooth. Refrigerate ganache 1 hour or until of a spreadable consistency.

2 Roll 20g (¾ ounce) of the ready-made icing into thin strips; brush with a little water. Sprinkle chocolate sprinkles onto icing to represent ants; gently push chocolate sprinkles into icing to secure.

Lay one of the jars on its side. Using picture as a guide, gently press strips of icing on inside surface of jar. Repeat to make a total of 6 jars.

3 Tint the coconut green (page 336). Divide cake crumbs evenly among jars; spread ganache over top of each jar, cover with coconut.

TIP You need about 2 x 600g (1¼-pound) packets chocolate cake to make the cake crumbs.

EQUIPMENT
- 6 X 1 CUP (250ML) CLEAR GLASS JARS

CAKE
- ¼ CUP (60ML) THICKENED (HEAVY) CREAM
- 100G (3 OUNCES) DARK CHOCOLATE, CHOPPED
- 8 CUPS (900G) CHOCOLATE CAKE CRUMBS (SEE TIP)

DECORATIONS
- 120G (4 OUNCES) READY-MADE WHITE ICING
- 1 TABLESPOON CHOCOLATE SPRINKLES
- 1 CUP (80G) DESICCATED COCONUT
- GREEN FOOD COLOURING

WRAPPED UP LIKE A MUMMY

EQUIPMENT
- 35CM (14-INCH) SQUARE CAKE BOARD (PAGE 332)

CAKE
- 1 X 453G (14½-OUNCE) TUB VANILLA FROSTING
- 12 X UNICED STANDARD CUPCAKES

DECORATIONS
- 400G (12½-OUNCE) PACKET MINTIES
- 24 RED MINI M&M'S

1 Spread frosting over top of cupcakes.

2 Unwrap Minties. Place one Mintie at a time on a small microwave-safe plate; heat in the microwave on medium-high (75%) for 5 seconds or until Mintie has softened. (Be careful as Minties may be very hot.)

3 When cool enough to handle, carefully stretch each Mintie, pulling it into thin strips. Cut strips into lengths long enough to fit across top of cupcakes. Lay strips of stretched Minties over cupcakes, overlapping to represent a mummy's bandage. Repeat with the remaining cupcakes and Minties.

4 Position M&Ms on cupcakes for eyes.

TIPS These cute little cupcakes would also be a welcome treat at a halloween party for younger children. If you can't find uniced cupcakes, use iced ones and trim the icing from the cupcakes.

THINGS THAT GO
BUMP
IN THE NIGHT

1 Preheat oven to 120°C/250°F. Line oven trays with baking paper.

2 To make meringue ghosts, beat egg white in a small bowl with an electric mixer until soft peaks form; gradually add sugar, beating until dissolved between additions. Beat in cornflour. Spoon meringue mixture into piping bag fitted with tube. Pipe about 36 meringue ghosts onto trays, ranging from 4cm (1½-inches) to 10cm (4-inches) in length, making pointed ends to push into muffins. Bake for 50 minutes or until dry and crisp. Cool meringues on trays. Pipe eyes and mouth onto cooled meringues with writing gel.

3 Spread frosting onto muffins. Using a small sharp knife, make incisions into muffins to insert ghosts. Using picture as a guide, decorate muffins with ghosts and fairy floss.

TIPS Meringue ghosts can be made 2 days ahead, store in an airtight container. Pipe eyes and mouth and insert ghosts into muffins on the day of serving.

EQUIPMENT
- **2 OVEN TRAYS**
- **LARGE PIPING BAG FITTED WITH A 7MM (¼-INCH) PLAIN TUBE**

CAKE
- **1 X 453G (14½-OUNCE) TUB VANILLA FROSTING**
- **12 DOUBLE CHOC-CHIP MUFFINS OR CUPCAKES**

DECORATIONS
- **1 EGG WHITE**
- **¼ CUP (55G) CASTER (SUPERFINE) SUGAR**
- **1 TEASPOON CORNFLOUR (CORNSTARCH)**
- **RED WRITING ICING OR GEL**
- **100G (3 OUNCES) WHITE VANILLA-FLAVOURED PERSIAN FAIRY FLOSS**

SUCCULENT GARDEN

FOR THESE RECIPES YOU WILL NEED 6 MINI UNICED CUPCAKES AND 3 TABLESPOONS READY-MADE VANILLA FROSTING. PLACE CUPCAKES INTO MINI POTS AND SPREAD TOPS WITH FROSTING. QUANTITIES GIVEN ARE ENOUGH TO DECORATE ONE CUPCAKE.

ALOE VERA

Sprinkle 2 teaspoons crushed chocolate biscuits over frosted cupcake. Slice green soft licorice into thirds lengthways; snip edges with kitchen scissors so they look 'spikey'. Using picture as a guide, position licorice in centre of pot.

SUCCULENT

Sprinkle 2 teaspoons crushed chocolate biscuits over frosted cupcake. Split 8 spearmint leaves in half horizontally. Using picture as a guide, position spearmint leaves, overlapping slightly, around centre of cupcake.

TOPIARY TREE

Sprinkle 2 teaspoons crushed chocolate biscuits over frosted cupcake. Tint 1 tablespoon frosting green; spoon into a small piping bag fitted with a 5mm (¼-inch) fluted tube. Push 1 pretzel stick into centre of cupcake; push 1 white marshmallow onto end of pretzel stick. Pipe small stars all over marshmallow to make topiary. Decorate with orange mini M&M's.

MONEY TREE

Sprinkle 2 teaspoons crushed chocolate biscuits over frosted cupcake. Secure 5 Mars Bar Pods together, upside-down, using a little melted milk chocolate. Refrigerate until set, then position in centre of cupcake for trunk, pushing into frosting. Cut 4 spearmint leaves in half horizontally. Using picture as a guide, position spearmint leaves, cut-side down onto trunk, securing with a little melted chocolate.

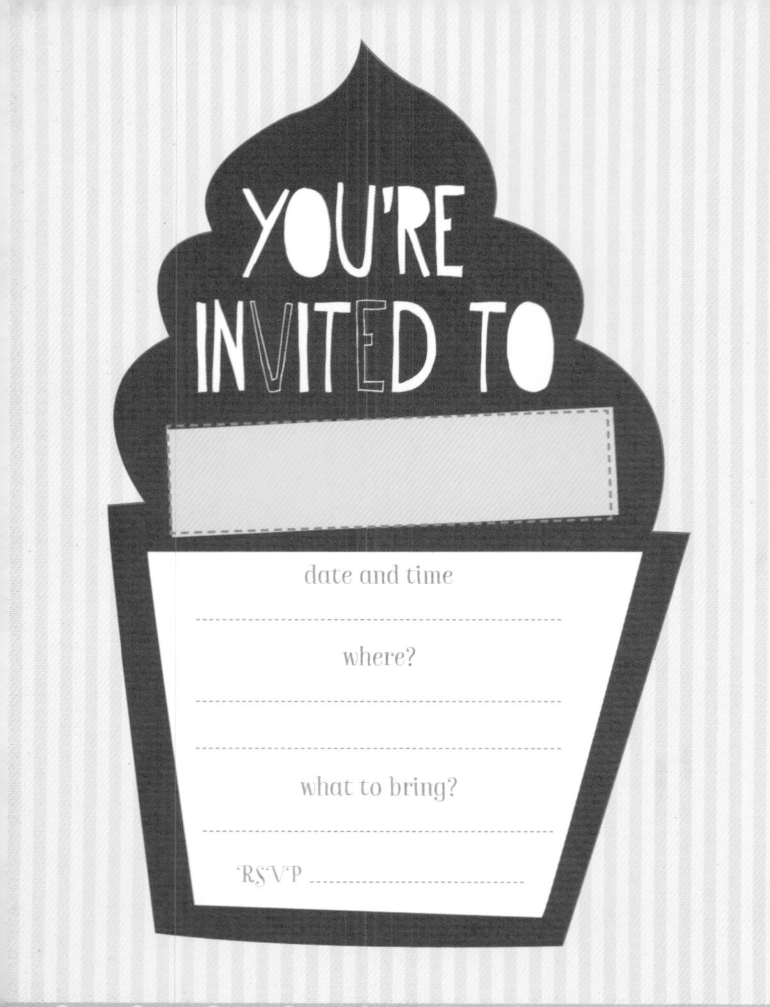

YOU'RE INVITED TO

date and time
....
where?
....
....
what to bring?
....
RSVP ....

YOU'RE INVITED TO

date and time
....
where?
....
....
what to bring?
....
RSVP ....

YOU'RE INVITED TO

date and time
....
where?
....
....
what to bring?
....
RSVP ....

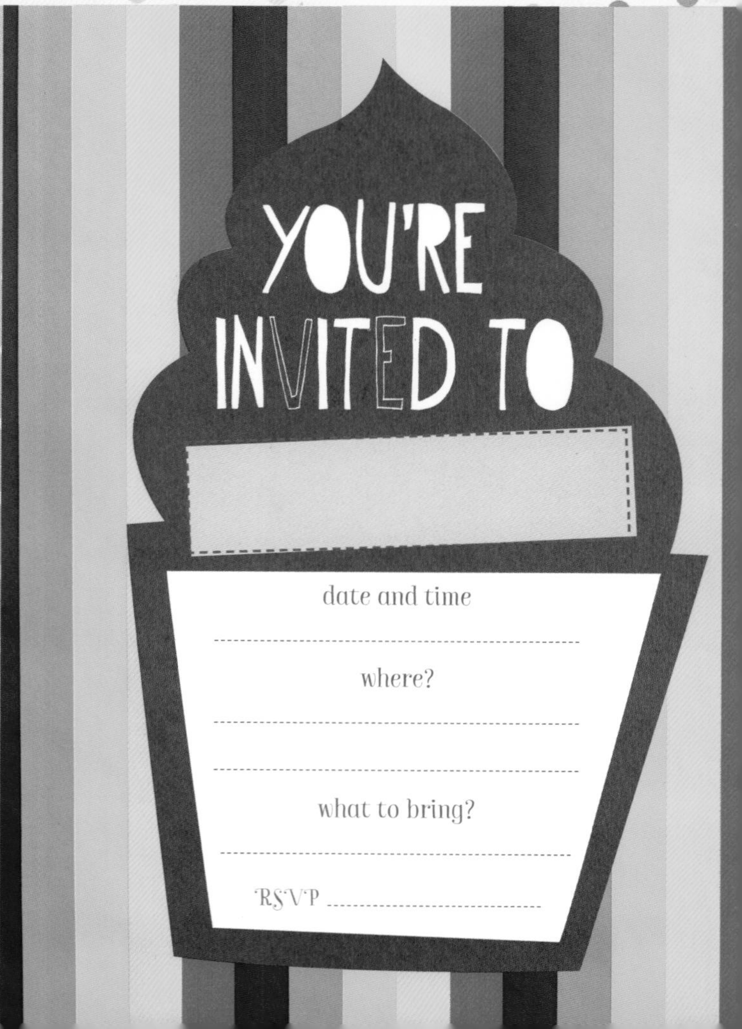

YOU'RE INVITED TO

date and time
....
where?
....
....
what to bring?
....
RSVP ....

JOIN US FOR

PARTY

DATE AND TIME

WHERE?

WHAT TO BRING?

RSVP

JOIN US FOR

PARTY

DATE AND TIME

WHERE?

WHAT TO BRING?

RSVP

JOIN US FOR

PARTY

DATE AND TIME

WHERE?

WHAT TO BRING?

RSVP

JOIN US FOR

PARTY

DATE AND TIME

WHERE?

WHAT TO BRING?

RSVP

Transport

THE WHEELS ON THE BUS

EQUIPMENT

- 30CM X 40CM (12-INCH X 16-INCH) RECTANGULAR CAKE BOARD (PAGE 332)

CAKE

- 1 X 453G (14½-OUNCE) TUB VANILLA FROSTING
- YELLOW FOOD COLOURING
- 2 X 515G (1 POUND) LOAF CAKES
- 2 X 42G (1½ OUNCE) MUFFIN BARS

DECORATIONS

- 1M (1 YARD) BLACK LICORICE STRAP
- 1 ROUND ORANGE JUBE, HALVED CROSSWAYS
- 4 CHOCOLATE CREAM-FILLED BISCUITS

1 Reserve ½ cup of the frosting. Tint remaining frosting yellow. Remove icing from tops of loaf cakes; level cake tops (page 333). Secure one cake, cut-side down, on cake board with a little frosting; spread cake top with ¼ cup of the yellow frosting. Top with remaining cake.

2 Using picture as a guide, stack and position muffin bars at one end of loaf cake to make front of bus, securing with a little yellow frosting.

3 Spread yellow frosting over top, front and bottom half of the bus, as pictured, but don't frost the window area; reserve about 1 tablespoon of the yellow frosting. Spread the reserved white frosting over top half of cake for bus windows.

4 Cut lengths of licorice strap and position around base of cake. Secure jubes to front of bus as headlights.

5 Cut remaining licorice strap into long thin strips; using picture as a guide, trim and position strips as windows. Using reserved frosting, secure biscuits to sides of cake for wheels.

TIP

We used black and brown chocolate rocks to decorate around the side of the road and in the 'park' area.

STOP

STOP

TIP

After turning the
first cake out of
the pan, wash the
cake pan and rinse
it in cold water then
dry, to remove any
residual heat.

BLASTOFF

1 Preheat oven to 180°C/350°F. Grease and flour cake pan (page 332).

2 Make one cake according to directions on packet. Spread mixture into pan; bake about 50 minutes. Stand cake in pan 10 minutes before turning, top-side up, onto a wire rack to cool. Repeat with second cake mix (see tip).

3 Using a serrated knife, level cake tops so cakes are the same height when placed side-by-side to form a rocket ship (one cake will be upside down, the other right-side up). Using picture as a guide, trim cake to resemble a rocket shape; secure to cake board with a little butter cream.

4 Tint butter cream violet; spread all over cake.

5 Decorate rocket with jelly beans; halve 7 white jelly beans crossways to make circle.

6 Position sparklers in cake; light sparklers just before serving.

EQUIPMENT

- 21CM X 32CM (8½-INCH X 12¾-INCH) NUMBER ONE CAKE PAN
- 35CM X 45CM (14-INCH X 18-INCH) RECTANGULAR CAKE BOARD (PAGE 332)

CAKE

- 2 X 340G (11-OUNCE) PACKETS BUTTER CAKE MIX
- 2 QUANTITIES BUTTER CREAM (PAGE 327)
- VIOLET FOOD COLOURING

DECORATIONS

- 4 X 190G (6-OUNCE) PACKETS JELLY BEANS
- 8 SPARKLERS

JELLY BEAN TRAIN

1 Preheat oven to 180°C/350°F. Grease cake pan (page 332); line base and sides with baking paper, extending paper 5cm (2-inch) above sides.

2 Make cakes according to directions on packets. Spread mixture into pan; bake about 1 hour. Stand cake in pan 10 minutes before turning, top-side up, onto a wire rack to cool. Using a serrated knife, level cake to 4cm (1½-inch) high.

3 Cut the cake into five 5cm x 5cm (2-inch) rectangles and one 2cm x 2cm (¾-inch) rectangle.

4 Divide butter cream into three small bowls; tint green, blue and yellow. Spread small cake and two larger cakes with green butter cream. Spread two larger cakes with blue butter cream and remaining cake with yellow butter cream.

5 Make engine by joining small cake and a blue cake on cake board. Arrange remaining carriages on board. Cut and discard tops off milk bottles. Use 4 milk bottles to join carriages together.

6 Using picture as a guide, decorate engine and carriages with Life Savers and jelly beans. Cut remaining milk bottles in half lengthways; position on either side of front carriage. Place candle at front of cake; slide peppermint Life Savers over candle.

EQUIPMENT
- DEEP 23CM (9¼-INCH) SQUARE CAKE PAN
- 40CM X 50CM (16-INCH X 20-INCH) RECTANGULAR CAKE BOARD (PAGE 332)

CAKE
- 3 X 340G (11-OUNCE) PACKETS BUTTER CAKE MIX
- 1 QUANTITY BUTTER CREAM (PAGE 327)
- GREEN, BLUE AND YELLOW FOOD COLOURING

DECORATIONS
- 5 WHITE MILK BOTTLES
- 1½ X 34G (1-OUNCE) PACKETS FIVE FLAVOURS LIFE SAVERS
- 24 JELLY BEANS
- 1 THIN BIRTHDAY CANDLE
- 4 PEPPERMINT LIFE SAVERS

TIPS

You need to purchase
2 x 420g (13½-ounce)
packets of muffin bars.
Use the sour straps
to decorate the petrol
tanker in a pattern
of your choice.

BIG RIG PETROL TANKER

1 Secure 8 muffin bars, side-by-side in a single line, on cake board with a little frosting. Secure sponge rolls on top of muffin bars with a little frosting.

2 Reserve ½ cup of the frosting. Tint remaining frosting yellow. Spread yellow frosting all over sponge rolls and muffin bars.

3 Position remaining muffins at front end of trailer to create driver's cab; secure with a little frosting. Tint reserved frosting grey with black colouring. Spread grey frosting all over sides and top of cab.

4 Unroll each licorice strap until you are left with a 6cm (2½-inch) diameter roll; trim away unrolled pieces. Cut licorice rolls in half to make 'wheels'. Position wheels on cake (you need 14 wheels). Secure Milkybar buttons to wheels with a little frosting. Trim remaining licorice to make two mud guards and windows; position on cab.

5 Cut two small stars from sour strap; position on cake as pictured. Using picture as a guide, decorate tanker with bootlaces. Cut 3 sour tubes in half crossways, position on cake to form front grill. Trim bootlace to fit across front of cab and back of tanker. Position orange M&M's as headlights and brake lights. Using picture as a guide, decorate cab with chocolate drops and yellow M&M's for rig lights. Attach remaining sour tubes as exhaust pipes.

EQUIPMENT

- 30CM X 40CM (12-INCH X 16-INCH) RECTANGULAR CAKE BOARD (PAGE 332)

CAKE

- 11 BANANA-FLAVOURED MUFFIN BARS (460G)
- 2 X 453G (14½-OUNCE) TUBS VANILLA FROSTING
- 2 X 500G (1-POUND) PACKETS HONEY SPONGE ROLLS
- YELLOW AND BLACK FOOD COLOURING

DECORATIONS

- 3½ X 240G (7½-OUNCE) PACKETS BLACK LICORICE STRAPS
- 14 MILKYBAR BUTTONS
- 1 RED SOUR STRAP
- 5 RED SOUR BOOTLACES
- 5 RED SOUR TUBES
- 4 ORANGE MINI M&M'S
- 2 YELLOW MINI CHOCOLATE DROPS
- 6 YELLOW MINI M&M'S

HEAVY LIFTER
ROAD CREW

EQUIPMENT

- 30CM X 40CM (12-INCH X 16-INCH) RECTANGULAR CAKE BOARD (PAGE 332)

CAKE

- 2 X 450G (14½-OUNCE) PACKAGED DOUBLE UNFILLED SPONGE SLABS
- 1 X 453G (14½-OUNCE) TUB DARK CHOCOLATE FROSTING

DECORATION

- 1 X 30G (1-OUNCE) BAR CHOCOLATE FLAKE
- 1 X 40G (1½-OUNCE) CHOCOLATE-COATED HONEYCOMB BAR, OR PLAIN HONEYCOMB
- 24 CHOCOLATE DROPS
- 20 BROWN MINI M&M'S
- ¼ CUP CHOCOLATE SPRINKLES
- ½ TEASPOON YELLOW NERDS
- SMALL TOY DIGGER TRUCKS AND CONSTRUCTION TOYS

1 Secure two of the cakes, side-by-side, on cake board with a little frosting. Spread frosting over top of cake. Cut remaining cakes into large pieces and stack on top of cake, securing with a little frosting. Using a small sharp knife; trim cake to form a mound.

2 Using a small serrated knife; cut into cake to create a 5cm (2-inch) wide sloping roadway around cake, leading to top of cake.

3 Spread cake all over with remaining frosting. Cut Flake into three pieces. Trim and discard chocolate coating from honeycomb; roughly chop honeycomb into small chunks.

4 Using picture as a guide, decorate cake with Flake, honeycomb, chocolate drops, M&M's, sprinkles and nerds. Position toys on cake.

TIPS You will need four slab cakes for this recipe. Sweets, such as Flake or chocolate-coated honeycomb, can be crushed and used as gravel on the road. If using butter cream instead of chocolate frosting, you will need two quantities of chocolate butter cream (page 327). Remember to remove all non-edible toys before serving.

TIPS

We used bottle lollies to keep with the recycle theme, but you can use mixed lollies, if you prefer. Small biodegradable seedling pots were used for the garbage bins.

RECYCLING TRANSPORTATION CHIEF

1 Secure one of the sponge cakes onto cake board with a little frosting. Place madeira cake on cake board at one short end of sponge cake; trim top of madeira cake so it is level with sponge cake (reserve trimmed cake piece). Secure madeira cake to cake board with a little frosting. Cut reserved madeira cake piece in half, diagonally lengthwise to form a wedge; place wedges on sponge cake at end closest to madeira cake. Secure remaining sponge cake on top of other sponge with a little frosting. It should sit on an angle with madeira wedges between sponge cakes.

2 Tint frosting blue. Spread frosting over top and sides of cake.

3 Reserve 8 chocolate Melts. Melt remaining chocolate (page 337). Secure reserved chocolate Melts to biscuits with a little of the melted chocolate. Spread remaining melted chocolate over one side of wafer. Set aside to set. Using picture as a guide, position biscuits and wafer onto cake.

4 Using picture as a guide, position mango twists, raspberry twists and M&M on cake. Attach two green licorice together; position for exhaust pipe.

5 Knead ready-made icing on a surface dusted with a little sifted icing sugar until it loses its stickiness. Roll icing until 3mm (⅛-inch) thick. Cut icing into 6 arrows, 4cm (1½-inch) long. Fold in half to make recycling symbol. Attach 3 on either side of cake.

6 Fill top of cake with remaining lollies, spilling over back of cake.

EQUIPMENT
- 30CM X 40CM (12-INCH X 16-INCH) RECTANGULAR CAKE BOARD (PAGE 332)

CAKE
- 1 X 450G (14½-OUNCE) PACKET DOUBLE UNFILLED SPONGE SLABS
- 2 X 453G (14½-OUNCE) TUBS VANILLA FROSTING
- 1 X 400G (12½-OUNCE) PACKET MADEIRA CAKE
- BLUE FOOD COLOURING

DECORATIONS
- 100G (3 OUNCES) WHITE CHOCOLATE MELTS
- 8 CHOCOLATE-FILLED CHOCOLATE BISCUITS
- 1 ICE-CREAM WAFER
- 4 MANGO FLAVOURED LICORICE TWISTS
- 5 RASPBERRY TWISTS
- 1 ORANGE PEANUT M&M, HALVED
- 2 GREEN SOFT EATING LICORICE
- 50G (1½ OUNCES) READY-MADE GREEN ICING
- PURE ICING (CONFECTIONERS') SUGAR, FOR DUSTING
- ½ X 170G (5½-OUNCE) PACKET MILK BOTTLES
- ½ X 175G (5½-OUNCE) PACKET FIZZY COLA BOTTLES
- ½ X 160G (5-OUNCE) PACKET LIQUID-FILLED COLA BOTTLE
- 6 BLUE SPRINKLE LICORICE ALLSORTS
- 2 CUPS COLOURED CANDY POPCORN

BALLOON
WITH A VIEW

1 Secure one of the cakes to cake board with a little frosting. Spread cake top with a little frosting; top with remaining cake. Using a small serrated knife; trim top edge of cake to create a dome shape. Spread frosting all over top and sides of cake.

2 Using picture as a guide, position marshmallows in coloured lines over cake.

3 Melt chocolate (page 337); cool slightly. Cut waffle basket in half crossways with a bread knife. Secure basket on its side, with a little melted chocolate, onto cake board.

4 Attach sour straps to basket with a little melted chocolate, push other end of straps into balloon.

TIPS You can also use raspberry and vanilla marshmallows, halved crossways, or a variety of chocolate buttons to decorate the balloon. If using butter cream instead of strawberry frosting, you will need one quantity of butter cream (page 327); you can tint it pink or leave it plain.

EQUIPMENT
- 30CM X 40CM (12-INCH X 16-INCH) RECTANGULAR CAKE BOARD (SEE 332)

CAKE
- 1 X 460G (14½-OUNCE) PACKAGED DOUBLE UNFILLED SPONGE CAKE ROUNDS
- 1 X 453G (14½-OUNCE) TUB STRAWBERRY FROSTING

DECORATIONS
- 2 X 175G (5½-OUNCE) PACKET BERRY DELIGHT MARSHMALLOW SWIRLS
- ¼ CUP (35G) WHITE CHOCOLATE MELTS
- 1 WAFFLE BASKET (15G)
- 3 RAINBOW SOUR STRAPS, YELLOW PART ONLY, TRIMMED INTO 3MM (1/8-INCH) THICK STRIPS

how to make
MINI BUNTING

Place on top of your cake like this!

Bunting is a cute and easy way to decorate your cake. All you have to do is cut out the diamonds, fold them in half, hang on a piece of string and glue the tips together. Hang the bunting between two skewers and insert into your cake.

YOU WILL NEED:

- SCISSORS
- GLUE STICK
- STRING

FOLD LINE

FOLD LINE

CUT

CAKE TOPPERS

Here are some decorating ideas for your crazy cake. Cut out the shapes, glue to a toothpick or bbq skewer and place in your cake or cupcake.

Playtime

SUPER-JUMPER'S SKIPPING ROPE

1 Secure cakes, long sides together, on cake board with a little frosting.

2 Reserve ½ cup of the frosting; tint remaining frosting green. Spread green frosting over top and sides of cake.

3 Tint the coconut green (page 336); press over top and sides of cake.

4 Divide ready-made icing in half. Knead half the icing on a surface dusted with a little sifted icing sugar until icing loses its stickiness. Tint remaining icing yellow; knead on a surface dusted with a little sifted icing sugar until icing loses its stickiness. Roll yellow icing into a rope shape about 60cm x 5mm (24-inch x ¼-inch) thick. Repeat with white icing. Twist both ropes together; gently

roll to secure together. Cut a little round from each end of rope, flatten slightly; reserve.

5 Place sprinkles in a shallow bowl. Spread remaining frosting all over both rollettes; roll in sprinkles to coat.

6 Using picture as a guide, position rollettes on cake to form skipping rope handles. Position rope on cake, gently pushing into end of each rollette; attach flattened icing ends on other side of rollettes to form rope knots.

TIPS If using butter cream instead of vanilla frosting, you will need two quantities of butter cream (page 327). You can use cream-filled rollettes, if you prefer. Use hundreds & thousands instead of orange sprinkles.

EQUIPMENT

- 30CM X 40CM (12-INCH X 16-INCH) RECTANGULAR CAKE BOARD (PAGE 332)

CAKE

- 1 X 450G (14½-OUNCE) PACKAGED DOUBLE UNFILLED SPONGE SLABS
- 1 X 453G (14½-OUNCE) TUB VANILLA FROSTING
- GREEN AND YELLOW FOOD COLOURING

DECORATIONS

- 3 CUPS (225G) MOIST COCONUT FLAKES
- 500G (1-POUND) READY-MADE WHITE ICING (PAGE 327)
- PURE ICING (CONFECTIONERS') SUGAR, FOR DUSTING
- ½ CUP ORANGE SPRINKLES
- 2 JAM ROLLETTES

GUMBALL MACHINES

EQUIPMENT

- OVEN TRAY
- PLASTIC WRAP
- 35CM (14-INCH) SQUARE CAKE BOARD (PAGE 332)

CAKE

- 1 X 450G (14½-OUNCE) PACKAGED DOUBLE UNFILLED SPONGE SLABS
- 1 X 453G (14½-OUNCE) TUB VANILLA FROSTING
- RED FOOD COLOURING
- 6 MINI DOUBLE CHOCOLATE MUFFINS

DECORATIONS

- 1 X 160G (5-OUNCE) PACKET MINI M&M'S
- RED WRITING ICING
- 6 WHITE CHOCOLATE MELTS

1 Blend or process cakes into crumbs. Combine cake crumbs and 1/3 cup of the frosting in a large bowl. Roll ½-cups of the mixture into six balls. Place on an oven tray; loosely cover with plastic wrap. Refrigerate 2 hours or until firm.

2 Divide remaining frosting into two bowls. Tint one bowl with red colouring. Remove paper cases from muffins; trim tops from muffins so they are flat. Spread base and sides of muffins with red frosting. Secure muffins, cut-side down, on cake board with a little frosting.

3 Place M&M's in a shallow bowl. Spread white frosting all over cake balls; roll cake balls evenly in M&M's to cover. Secure balls on top of muffins.

4 Use writing icing to pipe numbers on chocolate Melts (the number can be the birthday child's age). Secure buttons on muffins.

TIPS Use Skittles instead of mini M&M's. Store cakes in an airtight container in a cool dark place. Refrigerating cakes will cause the colour on the M&M's to run. If using butter cream instead of vanilla frosting, you will need one quantity of butter cream (page 327).

TIP

If you want a daytime scene, colour the frosting light blue and use a yellow jube as the sun and the sugar pearls to represent sun rays.

CITYSCAPE AT NIGHT

1 Secure cake to cake board with a little frosting.

2 Tint frosting dark blue with blue colouring. Reserve 1 tablespoon of the frosting; spread remaining over top and sides of cake.

3 Using picture as a guide, place licorice on cake to represent road. Cut biscuits into different lengths and widths to represent buildings; position on cake above road.

4 Spoon reserved frosting into piping bag. Pipe a few dots of frosting in some of the windows of the buildings and secure M&M's to biscuits for lights.

5 Place pearls above buildings for stars. Decorate with cars (see tip), if you like.

TIP We used car patches available from craft and sewing stores. You could use small diecast cars from toy shops. Be aware of choking hazards if using non-edible decorations and make sure they are removed before serving.

EQUIPMENT

- 25CM (10-INCH) SQUARE CAKE BOARD (PAGE 332)
- SMALL PIPING BAG FITTED WITH A SMALL PLAIN PIPING TUBE

CAKE

- 1 X 500G (1-POUND) PACKET CHOCOLATE BLOCK CAKE
- 1 X 453G (14½-OUNCE) TUB VANILLA FROSTING
- DARK BLUE FOOD COLOURING

DECORATIONS

- 20CM (8-INCH) PIECE BLACK LICORICE STRAP
- 4 LATTICE BISCUITS
- 13 YELLOW MINI M&M'S
- ½ TEASPOON YELLOW SOFT SUGAR PEARLS

TUBBY, THE WELL-ROUNDED BEAR

1 Secure one cinnamon doughnut to cake board with a little frosting, top with jam doughnut, securing with a little frosting; top with another cinnamon doughnut, secure with a little frosting.

2 Cut one cinnamon doughnut in half crossways. Spread a little frosting on one cut-side of each half; attach to body with a little frosting to form legs.

3 Cut another cinnamon doughnut in half crossways; secure to bear using toothpicks to form arms.

4 Using picture as a guide, position remaining cinnamon doughnut, upright, on top to form bear's head; secure with bamboo skewer.

5 Cut one-third from each mini doughnut; reserve one larger off-cut. Spread a little frosting over cut sides of smaller doughnuts; attach to head to form ears (secure with toothpicks if unstable). Trim one-third off end of an off-cut; use rounded end to form bear's nose, secure to face with a little frosting.

6 Using a little frosting, attach blue Smarties to head for eyes, and brown Smartie for a nose. Use writing gel to pipe mouth and pupils on bear. Use ribbon to make a bow; attach with a little frosting.

EQUIPMENT

- 20CM (8-INCH) ROUND CAKE BOARD (PAGE 332)
- 4 WOODEN TOOTHPICKS
- 1 SMALL BAMBOO SKEWER

CAKE

- 5 CINNAMON DOUGHNUTS
- 1 TABLESPOON READY-MADE VANILLA FROSTING
- 1 JAM DOUGHNUT
- 2 MINI DOUGHNUTS

DECORATIONS

- 2 BLUE SMARTIES
- 1 BROWN SMARTIE
- CHOCOLATE WRITING GEL
- 40CM X 1CM (16-INCH X ½-INCH) WIDE RIBBON

TIP

Be sure to remove
toothpicks and skewers
from cake before
cutting and serving.

ARTIST'S SKETCHBOOK

1 Level cake top (page 333). Secure cake, cut-side down, on cake board with a little frosting. Spread frosting over top and sides of cake.

2 Knead ready-made icing on a surface dusted with a little sifted icing sugar until icing loses its stickiness. Roll icing on a surface dusted with a little sifted icing sugar until large enough to cover cake (page 334).

3 Using a rolling pin, lift icing onto cake. Dust your hands lightly with icing sugar; smooth icing over cake. Trim icing neatly around base of cake; stand overnight to allow icing to firm.

4 Using coloured markers, let the kids go crazy and draw all over the cake themselves, or decorate with their favourite character.

TIPS If you prefer, you can buy food decorating pens online or at good cake decorating stores. If using butter cream instead of vanilla frosting, you will need one quantity of butter cream (page 327). Make this recipe a day ahead so that the ready-made icing dries hard enough to draw on.

EQUIPMENT

- 30CM (12-INCH) SQUARE CAKE BOARD (PAGE 332)

CAKE

- 20CM (8-INCH) SQUARE CAKE
- 1 X 453G (14½-OUNCE) TUB VANILLA FROSTING
- 2 X 500G (1-POUND) PACKETS READY-MADE WHITE ICING (PAGE 327)
- PURE ICING (CONFECTIONERS') SUGAR, FOR DUSTING

DECORATIONS

- NON-TOXIC EDIBLE COLOURED MARKERS

LAMINGTON CHECKERS

EQUIPMENT
- 40CM (16-INCH) SQUARE CAKE BOARD (PAGE 332)

CAKE
- 3 X 360G (11½-OUNCE) PACKETS LAMINGTONS

DECORATIONS
- 18 MINI CHOCOLATE CREAM-FILLED BISCUITS
- ½ X 453G (14½-OUNCE) TUB VANILLA FROSTING

1 Cut 18 lamingtons in half widthways. Using picture as guide, position lamingtons in a checkerboard pattern on cake board.

2 Spread tops of half the biscuits with frosting. Using picture as a guide, position biscuits on checkerboard.

TIP Pink lamingtons, available from supermarkets, would make a pretty pink checkerboard cake.

BALL SPORTS

1 Using cutter, cut six rounds from each cake. Spread frosting over tops of cake rounds.

2 Using picture as a guide, decorate cakes with M&M's, Tic Tacs and licorice to form ball patterns. Secure cakes to cake board with a little frosting.

TIPS Use a marble or butter cake, if you prefer. Double or triple the recipe to make more sport balls. For budding gardeners, turn these into garden beds by using M&M's to decorate the cakes as flowers.

EQUIPMENT
- 5CM (2-INCH) ROUND CUTTER
- 20CM (8-INCH) ROUND OR SQUARE CAKE BOARD (PAGE 332)

CAKE
- 2 X 500G (1-POUND) PACKETS CHOCOLATE BLOCK CAKE
- ½ X 453G (14½-OUNCE) TUB VANILLA FROSTING

DECORATIONS
- 32 ORANGE MINI M&M'S
- 56 RED MINI M&M'S
- 50 YELLOW MINI M&M'S
- 50 GREEN MINI M&M'S
- 42 WHITE TIC TACS
- 25CM (10-INCH) PIECE BLACK LICORICE STRAP, SLICED THINLY

CAMO CUPCAKES

EQUIPMENT

- 12-HOLE (⅓-CUP/80ML) STANDARD MUFFIN PAN
- 12 DARK GREEN PAPER CUPCAKE CASES
- 4 PAPER PIPING BAGS (PAGE 336)
- PLASTIC WRAP

CAKE

- 1 X 340G (11-OUNCE) PACKET BUTTER CAKE MIX
- ¼ CUP (25G) COCOA POWDER
- GOLDEN YELLOW, MOSS GREEN AND JUNIPER GREEN FOOD COLOURING
- 1 X 453G (14½-OUNCE) TUB VANILLA FROSTING
- COOKING-OIL SPRAY

1 Preheat oven to 180°C/350°F. Line muffin pan with paper cases.

2 Make cake according to directions on packet. Divide mixture evenly among four small bowls; tint one bowl dark brown using 3 teaspoons sifted cocoa; tint one bowl light brown using 1 teaspoon sifted cocoa and yellow colouring; tint one bowl dark green using 2 teaspoons sifted cocoa and moss green colouring; and tint remaining bowl of mixture light green using juniper green colouring.

3 Drop teaspoons of alternate-coloured mixtures into paper cases – you need to drop 10 teaspoons mixture into each paper case. Smooth surface; bake for about 15 minutes. Stand cakes in pan for 5 minutes before turning, top-side up, onto a wire rack to cool.

4 Divide frosting evenly among four small bowls; tint one bowl dark brown using 3 teaspoons sifted cocoa; tint one bowl light brown using 1 teaspoon sifted cocoa and yellow colouring; tint one bowl dark green using 2 teaspoons sifted cocoa and moss green colouring; and tint remaining bowl light green using juniper green colouring.

5 Place each colour frosting into a piping bag; snip ends to make a 5mm (¼-inch) opening. Using picture as a guide, pipe frosting, in random spots, over cupcakes to create a camouflage pattern.

6 Lightly spray cooking oil over a small piece of plastic wrap. Place plastic wrap, oiled-side down, over a cupcake and press lightly to flatten frosting. Remove plastic; repeat with remaining cupcakes.

TIP

We made the cupcakes so we could tint the mixture in camouflage colours. To save time, decorate store-bought cupcakes with the camouflage frosting.

TIPS

We used one double unfilled sponge to make 4 cups cake crumbs. This recipe is easy to double or triple. If using butter cream instead of vanilla frosting, you will need one quantity of butter cream (page 327).

ICE-CREAM SUNDAES

1 Place cake crumbs in a large bowl. Add ½ cup of the vanilla frosting; stir to combine. Roll 2/3 cups of the mixture into eight balls. Place on oven tray; loosely cover with plastic wrap. Refrigerate 2 hours or until firm.

2 Place remaining vanilla frosting in a microwave-safe jug. Microwave frosting on high (100%) for 10 seconds or until melted slightly. Carefully pour frosting over balls; stand until frosting sets slightly. Place balls in wafer baskets. Secure baskets to cake board with a little frosting.

3 Place chocolate frosting in a microwave-safe jug. Microwave frosting on high (100%) for 10 seconds or until melted slightly. Carefully pour chocolate frosting over balls; scatter with hundreds & thousands, then top with cherries.

EQUIPMENT
- OVEN TRAY
- PLASTIC WRAP
- 20CM (8-INCH) ROUND OR SQUARE CAKE BOARD (PAGE 332)

CAKE
- 8 CUPS (900G) CAKE CRUMBS (SEE TIPS)
- 2 X 453G (14½-OUNCE) TUBS VANILLA FROSTING
- 8 ICE-CREAM WAFFLE BASKETS
- ½ CUP (170G) CHOCOLATE FROSTING

DECORATIONS
- 2 TABLESPOONS HUNDREDS & THOUSANDS
- 8 RED GLACÉ CHERRIES

A FROSTY WINTER'S CASTLE

EQUIPMENT

- 35CM (14-INCH) ROUND CAKE BOARD (PAGE 332)
- 8CM (3¼-INCH) ROUND CUTTER
- 3 LONG BAMBOO SKEWERS

CAKE

- 1½ X 460G (14½-OUNCE) PACKAGED DOUBLE UNFILLED SPONGE CAKE ROUNDS
- 2 X 453G (14½-OUNCE) TUBS VANILLA FROSTING
- 1 X 250G (8-OUNCE) PACKET JAM ROLLETTES

DECORATIONS

- 3 MINI WAFFLE ICE-CREAM CONES
- 1 CUP (80G) DESICCATED COCONUT
- 3 FLAG CAKE TOPPERS
- 2 ICE-CREAM WAFERS
- 8 X 250G (8-OUNCE) PACKETS MARSHMALLOWS (SEE TIP)

1 Secure one cake to cake board with a little frosting. Reserve ¼ cup of the frosting. Sandwich second cake on top of cake on board with a little frosting. Spread top and sides with half the remaining frosting.

2 Place cutter on top of remaining cake; using cutter as a guide, cut an 8cm (3¼-inch) round from cake. Place cake round in centre of iced cake; spread top and sides with frosting.

3 Thread three jam rollettes onto a bamboo skewer. Repeat with remaining rollettes to make three towers. Spread top and sides with remaining frosting. Arrange towers around base of cake.

4 Place reserved frosting in a microwave-safe bowl. Microwave frosting on medium (50%) for 10 seconds or until melted slightly; drizzle over top of cones. Sprinkle with coconut. Gently push cake topper into top of each cone. Position cones on top of each tower.

5 Cut wafers into door and window shapes. Using picture as a guide, decorate cake with marshmallows. Position wafer door and windows, securing with a little frosting as necessary.

TIP

We only used the white marshmallows from the packets of marshmallows; serve the pink marshmallows at the party. You can make the castle pink and white, if you like; in this case you will only need 4 packets of marshmallows.

PIRATE'S TREASURE

1 Using a small sharp knife, cut peak off top of each muffin; reserve. Dig about 1 tablespoon cake out of centre of each muffin; discard.

2 Divide mixed lollies evenly into centre of each muffin, filling almost to the top. Top with reserved muffin tops, trimming so they fit snugly in hole on top of lollies.

3 Tint frosting green; spread over tops of muffins.

4 Discard chocolate from honeycomb; break honeycomb into pieces. Using picture as a guide, decorate cakes with honeycomb and assorted pirate toys. On one cake draw an 'X' with decorating icing using a flat piping nozzle (these come with the icing tube). Position cakes on cake board; secure with a little frosting.

TIPS You will need 3 x 4-pack (460g) double chocolate chip muffins for this cake. We used a selection of small jelly beans, rainbow choc chips and M&M's for the treasure. If using butter cream instead of vanilla frosting, you will need half a quantity of butter cream (page 327). If using non-edible decorations, make sure they are removed before serving.

EQUIPMENT

- 40CM (16-INCH) SQUARE CAKE BOARD (PAGE 332)

CAKE

- 12 DOUBLE CHOCOLATE CHIP MUFFINS
- 1 X 453G (14½-OUNCE) TUB VANILLA FROSTING
- GREEN FOOD COLOURING

DECORATIONS

- 1½ CUPS SMALL MIXED LOLLIES
- 1 X 50G (1½-OUNCE) CHOCOLATE-COATED HONEYCOMB BAR, OR PLAIN HONEYCOMB
- ASSORTED PIRATE TOYS
- RED DECORATING ICING

I CAN SEE A RAINBOW

EQUIPMENT

- 12-HOLE (1/3-CUP/80ML) STANDARD MUFFIN PAN
- 12 COLOURED PAPER MUFFIN CASES
- 6 SMALL ZIPTOP PLASTIC BAGS

CAKE

- 1 X 340G (11-OUNCE) PACKET BUTTER CAKE MIX
- RED, YELLOW, GREEN, ORANGE, PURPLE AND BLUE FOOD COLOURING
- 1 X 453G (14½-OUNCE) TUB VANILLA FROSTING

DECORATIONS

- RED, YELLOW, GREEN, ORANGE, PURPLE AND BLUE SPRINKLES

1 Preheat oven to 160°C/325°F. Line muffin pan with paper cases.

2 Make cake according to directions on packet. Divide mixture evenly between 6 bowls and tint red, yellow, green, orange, purple and blue. Spoon each colour into a separate ziptop bag; snip off a corner. Pipe red cake mixture into centre of each paper case. Push corner of yellow ziptop bag into centre of red cake mix and pipe in yellow cake mixture. Repeat with remaining green, orange, purple and blue mixtures. Bake about 15 minutes; stand cakes in pan 5 minutes before turning, top-side up, onto a wire rack to cool.

3 Divide frosting into 6 small bowls; tint red, yellow, green, orange, purple and blue. Spread a different colour frosting over two of the cupcakes; then using picture as a guide, decorate cupcakes with matching sprinkles.

TIPS We used paper cases to match each colour of the cupcakes. We made the cupcakes instead of buying them so we could tint the mixture in rainbow colours. To save time, decorate tops of store-bought cupcakes with the rainbow frostings.

TIP

To decorate the
cake board with sand,
colour 2 cups desiccated
coconut with yellow food
colouring (page 336).

GROMMET'S SURFBOARD

1 Position cakes on cake board so short ends of sponge are together.

2 Using a small serrated knife, trim sides of cake to form a surfboard shape. Secure to cake board with a little frosting. Discard trimmed pieces.

3 Spread frosting over top and sides of cake.

4 Melt chocolate (page 337). Cool slightly.

5 Using picture as a guide, position bootlaces down centre of board, trim to fit. Brush sour straps with a little water to remove sugar; position across surfboard on a slight angle, trim to fit. Position licorice strap at end of cake to create a leg rope, secure with a little melted chocolate.

6 Cut each white milk bottle lengthways into three pieces; position five pieces on rainbow strap to form a flower shape; cut top from yellow milk bottle; secure to middle of flower with a little melted chocolate.

EQUIPMENT

- 30CM X 40CM (12-INCH X 16-INCH) RECTANGULAR CAKE BOARD (PAGE 332)

CAKE

- 1 X 450G (14½-OUNCE) PACKAGED DOUBLE UNFILLED SPONGE SLABS
- 1 X 453G (14½-OUNCE) TUB VANILLA FROSTING

DECORATIONS

- 20G (¾ OUNCE) DARK CHOCOLATE MELTS
- 1 RED SOUR BOOTLACE
- 2 YELLOW SOUR BOOTLACES
- 3 RAINBOW SOUR STRAPS
- 120CM (48-INCH) PIECE BLACK LICORICE STRAP, TRIMMED TO 3MM (⅛-INCH) THICK
- 2 WHITE MILK BOTTLES
- 1 YELLOW MILK BOTTLE

SPRINGTIME DELIGHT

EQUIPMENT

- **TWO DEEP 18CM (7¼-INCH) ROUND CAKE PANS**
- **22CM (8¾-INCH) ROUND CAKE BOARD (PAGE 332)**

CAKE

- **2 X 340G (11-OUNCE) PACKETS BUTTER CAKE MIX**
- **¼ CUP (80G) RASPBERRY JAM (CONSERVE), WARMED, STRAINED, COOLED**
- **2 QUANTITIES BUTTER CREAM (PAGE 327)**

DECORATIONS

- **24 STRAWBERRIES & CREAM LOLLIES**
- **6 CARAMEL MILK BOTTLES**
- **12 JAFFAS**
- **PINK EDIBLE GLITTER DUST**
- **1.6 METRES (63-INCH) RIBBON, APPROXIMATELY**
- **PAPER SCRAPBOOKING FLOWERS**

1 Preheat oven to 180°C/350°F. Grease cake pans (page 332); line bases with baking paper.

2 Make cakes according to directions on packets. Spread mixture evenly into cake pans; bake about 1 hour. Stand cakes in pans 10 minutes before turning, top-side up, onto wire racks to cool.

3 Using a serrated knife, level cake tops (page 333). Sandwich cakes together with jam; secure on cake board with a little butter cream.

4 Cover cake all over with butter cream.

5 Trim edge off strawberries & cream to make wings of butterflies; join two trimmed edges together using picture as a guide. Position wings on cake with milk bottles as body; push into butter cream to secure. Decorate cake with Jaffas. Sprinkle cake with glitter dust. Tie ribbon around base of cake, and attach paper flowers.

It's always the right time to play a game. We can set up the board and play checkers, snakes and ladders or scrabble. Or let's go to the beach and play football.

OOPS, I DID IT AGAIN!

1 Secure cakes, long sides together, on cake board with a little frosting. Shape cake if necessary into a book shape (see tip). Spread frosting over top and sides of cake.

2 Draw lines on cake with blue writing icing.

3 Cut blueberry and raspberry licorice tubes into desired length for pens; trim one end into a point using a small sharp knife. Pipe a little blue and red decorating icing on points of each lolly for pen nibs.

4 Place black licorice strip down middle of cake. Decorate base of cake with sour straps trimming to fit around cake. Outline top of sour strap with red writing icing.

5 Using green and red writing icing, and picture as a guide, decorate cake; you could make it a maths book, as we have done here, or write a poem, a short story or draw pictures on the book.

TIP Look for cakes with slightly domed tops, otherwise you will have to trim the cake tops to create the curved book shape.

EQUIPMENT
- 30CM X 40CM (12-INCH X 16-INCH) RECTANGULAR CAKE BOARD (PAGE 332)
- BAMBOO SKEWER

CAKE
- 1 X 450G (14½-OUNCE) PACKAGED DOUBLE UNFILLED SPONGE SLABS
- 1 X 453G (14½-OUNCE) TUB VANILLA FROSTING

DECORATIONS
- BLUE, RED, GREEN WRITING ICING
- 3 BLUEBERRY LICORICE TUBES
- 1 RASPBERRY LICORICE TUBE
- BLUE AND RED DECORATING ICING
- 40CM (16-INCH) PIECE BLACK LICORICE, CUT INTO A THIN STRIP
- 6 RED SOUR STRAPS

HOPSCOTCH

1 Preheat oven to 180°C/350°F. Grease lamington pan; line base and long sides with baking paper, extending paper 5cm (2-inch) above sides.

2 Make cakes according to directions on packets. Spread mixture into pan; bake about 35 minutes. Stand cake in pan 5 minutes before turning, top-side up, onto a wire rack to cool.

3 Divide butter cream into three small bowls; Tint each bowl a different shade of grey using black colouring.

4 Using a serrated knife, level cake top; turn cake cut-side down. Trim cake to 14cm x 28cm (5½-inch x 11¼-inch). Using picture as a guide, cut home shape from cake. Cut remaining cake into eight 7cm (2¾-inch) squares.

5 Spread cakes all over with different shades of grey butter cream. Secure cakes to cake board with a little butter cream.

6 Trim snakes to make numbers one to eight, secure to cakes. Arrange and trim remaining lollies to make the word 'HOME', secure to cake.

EQUIPMENT

- 20CM X 30CM (8-INCH X 12-INCH) LAMINGTON PAN
- 20CM X 50CM (8-INCH X 20-INCH) RECTANGULAR CAKE BOARD (PAGE 332)

CAKE

- 2 X 340G (11-OUNCE) PACKETS BUTTER CAKE MIX
- 2½ QUANTITIES BUTTER CREAM (PAGE 327)
- BLACK FOOD COLOURING

DECORATIONS

- 8 JELLY SNAKES
- 5 HONEY BEARS
- 1 PEACHES & CREAM LOLLY
- 1 RED FROG
- 1 RACING CAR

HOME

7 8

6

4 5

3

2

1

TIP
Honey bears, peaches
& cream, frogs and
racing cars can be
found in packets
of party mix.

SNAKES & ROPES

1 Preheat oven to 180°C/350°F. Line muffin pans with cupcake cases.

2 Make cakes according to directions on packets. Drop 2½ level tablespoons of the mixture into each paper case; bake about 20 minutes. Stand cakes in pans 5 minutes before turning, top-side up, onto wire racks to cool.

3 Place half the butter cream into a small bowl; tint green. Tint remaining butter cream blue.

4 Spoon green butter cream into piping bag, pipe onto half the cakes. Repeat with blue butter cream (see tips).

5 Using picture as a guide, secure cakes on cake board with a little butter cream.

6 Place a chocolate melt into the corner of each cake; using piping gel, pipe numbers 1 to 36 on chocolate Melts. Decorate cakes with snakes and nerds ropes.

TIPS Wash and dry the piping tube between colours. You can use melted dark chocolate Melts (page 327) to pipe the numbers, instead of using chocolate piping gel.

EQUIPMENT
- 3 X 12-HOLE (⅓-CUP/80ML) STANDARD MUFFIN PANS
- 36 SQUARE CUPCAKE CASES
- 2 DISPOSABLE PIPING BAGS FITTED WITH A 1CM (½-INCH) PLAIN PIPING TUBE
- 45CM (18-INCH) SQUARE CAKE BOARD (PAGE 332)

CAKE
- 3 X 340G (11-OUNCE) PACKETS BUTTER CAKE MIX
- 2 QUANTITIES BUTTER CREAM (PAGE 327)
- GREEN AND BLUE FOOD COLOURING

DECORATIONS
- 36 WHITE CHOCOLATE MELTS
- CHOCOLATE PIPING GEL
- 5 JELLY SNAKES
- 3½ X 25G (¾-OUNCE) PACKETS NERDS ROPES

PIGGY
THE MONEY MAKER

EQUIPMENT
- 9.5CM (4-INCH) ROUND CUTTER
- 30CM (12-INCH) ROUND CAKE BOARD (PAGE 332)

CAKE
- ½ X 460G (1¼-POUND) PACKAGED DOUBLE UNFILLED SPONGE CAKE ROUND (YOU ONLY NEED 1 CAKE)
- 1 X 453G (14½-OUNCE) TUB STRAWBERRY FROSTING
- 2 X MINI JAM ROLLETTES

DECORATIONS
- 4 X 80G (2½-OUNCE) BAGS GOLD-FOIL COVERED CHOCOLATE COINS
- 1 WHITE MARSHMALLOW
- 1 BLACK LICORICE STICK
- 1 PINK MINI MARSHMALLOW
- 6 WHITE M&M'S
- 1 RED SOUR STRAP
- 3CM (1¼-INCH) PIECE LICORICE STRAP

1 Using cutter, cut a round from cake (cut from lower third of cake, not centre). Carefully lift out cut cake; reserve. Position larger cake piece on cake board, securing with a little frosting.

2 Fill hole in larger cake with chocolate coins, reserving 4-5 coins for decoration.

3 Carefully position reserved cake round on top of coins. Cut 1 jam rollette in half on the diagonal; using a little frosting, secure against bottom of cake for trotters.

4 Cut a 1.5cm (¾-inch) slice from remaining jam rollette; position on cake for snout, secure with a little frosting. Cut remaining piece of jam rollette in half on the diagonal; position on cake for ears, securing with a little frosting.

5 Spread remaining frosting all over cake. Cut white marshmallow in half; position on cake, cut-side up, for eyes. Cut black licorice stick into thin rounds, secure to marshmallows for eyes. Cut mini marshmallow in half, position on snout. Position M&M's on trotters.

6 Cut triangles from sour strap; position on ears. Cut a 1cm x 3cm (½-inch x 1¼-inch) oval shape from licorice strap; position on top of cake for coin slot. Position reserved coins around edge of cake.

WELCOME TO CANDY LAND

EQUIPMENT

- 30CM X 40CM (12-INCH X 16-INCH) RECTANGULAR CAKE BOARD (PAGE 332)

CAKE

- 2 X 450G (14½-OUNCE) PACKETS DOUBLE UNFILLED SPONGE SLABS
- 1½ X 453G (14½-OUNCE) TUBS VANILLA FROSTING
- 1 X CHOCOLATE CHIP MUFFIN
- 1 X MINI CHOCOLATE CHIP MUFFIN

DECORATIONS

- 3 WIZZ FIZZ SHERBET CONES
- 2 FLAT-BASED ICE-CREAM CONES
- 1 MINI ICE-CREAM CONE
- 1 RED SOUR STRAP
- 22 JELLY SWEETHEARTS
- 24 SMALL PINK BOILED LOLLIES
- 1 YELLOW JUBE
- 1 RED BOILED LOLLY
- 3 FLAG CAKE TOPPERS
- 7 ORANGE, PINK AND GREEN LICORICE ALLSORTS, HALVED
- 32 PINK MINI MARSHMALLOWS
- 29 MUSK STICKS
- 1½ NECKLACE LOLLIES
- 6 COCONUT ICE, CHOPPED
- 2 TABLESPOONS RAINBOW SUGAR PEARLS
- 3 LARGE FLAT LOLLIPOPS, STICKS TRIMMED
- 3 SMALL ROUND LOLLIPOPS, STICKS TRIMMED
- 3 PINK DOMED MARSHMALLOWS
- 8 PINK SPRINKLE LICORICE ALLSORTS

1 Secure two of the cakes, long sides together, on cake board with a little frosting. Top with remaining cakes. Position muffins at one corner of cake. Reserve 2 teaspoons of the frosting. Spread remaining frosting over top and sides of cake and muffins.

2 Trim top off one of the sherbet cones; press cone onto mini muffin. Press one of the flat-based cones onto large muffin then top with mini ice-cream cone. Position remaining flat-based cone next to muffins. Cut red sour strap to make door; position onto large muffin. Position remaining sherbet cones on either side of door. Press hearts onto sides of muffins then position a row of pink boiled lollies above hearts.

3 Secure jube on top of red boiled lolly with a little reserved frosting. Place on top of the flat base cone. Top with flags.

4 Using picture as a guide, decorate cake with remaining lollies.

TIP Remove any non-edible decorations before serving.

SAND BUCKET
AT THE BEACH

YOU NEED TO MAKE THE BEACH SHAPES THE DAY BEFORE THE CAKE AS THEY MUST DRY OVERNIGHT.

EQUIPMENT

- BEACH-THEMED CHOCOLATE MOULDS
- COOKING-OIL SPRAY
- 15CM (6-INCH), 16CM (6½-INCH) AND 30CM (12-INCH) ROUND CAKE BOARDS (PAGE 332)
- 4 WOODEN SKEWERS
- 2 WOODEN TOOTHPICKS

CAKE

- 1½ X 450G (14½-OUNCE) PACKETS DOUBLE UNFILLED SPONGE CAKE ROUNDS
- 2 X 453G (14½-OUNCE) TUBS VANILLA FROSTING
- RED FOOD COLOURING

DECORATIONS

- 125G (4 OUNCES) READY-MADE YELLOW ICING
- PURE ICING (CONFECTIONERS') SUGAR, FOR DUSTING
- 185G (6 OUNCES) READY-MADE WHITE ICING
- BLUE AND ORANGE FOOD COLOURING
- 250G (8 OUNCES) MILK ARROWROOT BISCUITS

1 Spray chocolate moulds with cooking oil. Knead ready-made yellow icing on a surface dusted with a little sifted icing sugar until icing loses its stickiness. Divide into small pieces and press into some of the holes in chocolate moulds. Reserve 60g of the ready-made white icing. Divide remaining white icing into 2 portions; tint one portion blue and other portion orange. Divide icing into small pieces and press into remaining holes in chocolate moulds. Stand moulds overnight to harden. Remove beach shapes from moulds.

2 Using cake boards as guides, cut one of the cake layers into a 15cm (6-inch) round. Cut one of the remaining cake layers into a 16cm (6½-inch) round. Secure 15cm (6-inch) cake to 30cm (12-inch) cake board with a little frosting.

Spread cake with a little frosting then top with the 16cm (6½-inch) cake. Spread cake with a little frosting and top with remaining uncut cake. Trim skewers to height of cake and push through centre of cakes to secure layers. Place cake in freezer until firm.

3 Tint frosting red and spread over top and side of cake.

4 Knead reserved white icing on a surface dusted with a little sifted icing sugar until icing loses its stickiness. Roll icing into a 25cm (10-inch) rope. Using picture as a guide, secure each end of rope to cake with toothpicks.

5 Process biscuits until coarse crumbs form. Sprinkle crumbs over top and around base of bucket. Place beach shapes on top and around bucket.

TIPS

The beach shapes can be made a week ahead; store in an airtight container at room temperature. Remember to remove the toothpicks and skewers before serving the cake.

TIP
Any leftover lollies
can be used in lolly bags
or in a piñata.

SCARY MNTRS

1 Cut cake into six 6cm (2½-inch) squares. Divide frosting into three bowls. Tint one bowl grey with black colouring and one bowl green with green colouring; leave remaining bowl white. Spread two cakes with each colour.

2 Using picture as a guide, decorate monster faces with lollies, cutting lollies as required.

EQUIPMENT
- 30CM (12-INCH) RECTANGULAR CAKE BOARD (PAGE 332)

CAKE
- 500G (1-POUND) CHOCOLATE BLOCK CAKE
- 1 X 453G (14½-OUNCE) TUB VANILLA FROSTING
- BLACK AND GREEN FOOD COLOURING

DECORATIONS

GREY MONSTER
- 4 SUGAR-FREE DOUBLE D PINK JELLY ROUNDS
- 4 JELLY TEETH
- 2 MUSK STICKS, HALVED
- 2 BLACK LICORICE STICKS

GREEN MONSTER
- 6 GREEN LOLLIPOPS
- 6 WHITE MARSHMALLOWS
- 3 BLACK LICORICE STICKS
- 2 RED SOUR FRUIT RINGS

WHITE MONSTER
- 16CM (6½ INCHES) LICORICE STRAP
- 1 BLACK LICORICE STICK
- 2 BROWN MINI M&M'S
- 2 YELLOW SOUR FRUIT RINGS
- 3CM PIECE (1¼ INCH) RED SOUR STRAP, HALVED
- 8CM PIECE (3¼ INCH) RAINBOW SOUR STRAP (BLUE PART ONLY), HALVED

FUN WITH LETTERS

EQUIPMENT

- 30CM (12-INCH) ROUND CAKE BOARD (PAGE 332)

CAKE

- 2 X 600G (1¼-POUND) PACKETS ROUND CARAMEL MUD CAKES
- 1 X 453G (14½-OUNCE) TUB VANILLA FROSTING

DECORATIONS

- RED, BLUE, GREEN AND YELLOW WRITING ICING
- 6 X 21G (¾-OUNCE) PACKETS LETTER JUMBLES BISCUITS (MINI MILK ARROWROOT BISCUITS)
- 33 M&M'S (RED, BLUE, GREEN AND YELLOW)
- 15 MINI M&M'S (RED, BLUE, GREEN AND YELLOW)
- RED, BLUE, GREEN AND YELLOW CANDLES

1 Remove icing from cakes; level cakes (page 333). Secure one cake, cut-side down, on cake board with a little frosting. Spread cake with ¼ cup of the frosting; top with remaining cake. Spread top and side of cake with frosting.

2 Using picture as a guide, use writing icings to decorate letters on biscuits; position on cakes (try not to have two biscuits with the same colour or letter next to each other).

3 Using picture as a guide, position M&M's and mini M&M's on cake to fill gaps between biscuits. Position candles on cake.

TIP Letter jumbles are sold in multi packs. You can use small plain round biscuits and write letters on them, if you prefer.

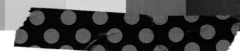

COLIN
THE CLOWN

1   Preheat oven to 180°C/350°F. Grease cake pans; line bases with baking paper (page 332).

2   Make cakes according to directions on packets. Divide mixture evenly between pans; bake about 1 hour. Stand cakes in pans 5 minutes before turning, top-side up, onto wire racks to cool.

3   Using a serrated knife, level cake tops so they are same height. Turn cakes cut-side down. For clown's hat, mark a point halfway along top edge of square cake; cut from this point to bottom corners to form a large triangle, reserve triangle for hat. For clown's bow tie, using picture as a guide, cut two even-sided triangles from leftover square cake; discard any remaining cake.

4   Secure round cake, cut-side down, on cake board with a little butter cream; position and secure cake triangles on board to form hat and bow tie.

5   Place half the butter cream in a medium bowl; tint yellow. Place half the remaining butter cream in a small bowl, tint blue. Tint remaining butter cream purple.

6   Spread yellow butter cream all over clown's face, spread blue butter cream over hat and spread purple butter cream over bow tie.

7   Bend nerds ropes; place around face for hair. Position white chocolate Melts on face to make eyes; attach blue Smarties with a little butter cream. Place thinly sliced jelly babies around eyes.

8   To make nose, secure Jaffa on freckle with a little butter cream; position on face. Position raspberries and lollipops for cheeks and ears. Trim snakes into a mouth shape; position on cake with teeth inside.

9   Decorate bow tie with Smarties, and hat with jubes.

EQUIPMENT

- DEEP 20CM (8-INCH) SQUARE CAKE PAN
- DEEP 22CM (8¾-INCH) ROUND CAKE PAN
- 30CM X 60CM (12-INCH X 24-INCH) RECTANGULAR CAKE BOARD (PAGE 332)

CAKE

- 3 X 340G (11-OUNCE) PACKETS BUTTER CAKE MIX
- 2 QUANTITIES BUTTER CREAM (PAGE 327)
- YELLOW, BLUE AND PURPLE FOOD COLOURING

DECORATIONS

- 2 X 25G (¾-OUNCE) PACKETS NERDS ROPE
- 2 WHITE CHOCOLATE MELTS
- 2 BLUE SMARTIES
- 2 CHOCOLATE JELLY BABIES, SLICED THINLY
- 1 JAFFA
- 1 CHOCOLATE FRECKLE
- 2 JELLY RASPBERRIES
- 2 GREEN LOLLIPOPS
- 2 RED JELLY SNAKES
- 1 JELLY TEETH
- 12 SMARTIES
- 16 JUBES

LOLLY FACES

EQUIPMENT

- 12-HOLE (⅓-CUP/80ML) STANDARD MUFFIN PAN
- 12 PAPER MUFFIN CASES

CAKE

- 1 X 340G (11-OUNCE) PACKET BUTTER CAKE MIX
- 1 QUANTITY BUTTER CREAM (PAGE 327)

DECORATIONS

- 14 SMARTIES
- 4 JELLY SNAKES
- 6 CHOCOLATE FRECKLES
- 2 COLA BOTTLES
- 2 JELLY LIPS
- 2 JELLY TEETH
- 1 PINEAPPLE
- 1 HONEY BEAR
- 2 JELLY RASPBERRIES
- 7 FRUIT TINGLES LIFE SAVERS

1 Preheat oven to 180°C/350°F. Line muffin pan with paper cases.

2 Make cake according to directions on packet. Spread ¼ cup of the mixture into each hole; bake about 20 minutes. Stand cakes in pan 5 minutes before turning, top-side up, onto a wire rack to cool.

3 Spread cakes evenly with butter cream. Using picture as a guide, decorate cakes using lollies to make funny faces.

TIPS All the lollies used here have been cut into various sizes and shapes to resemble mouths, eyes, ears and noses; for example, snakes can be cut into smiles, the heads can be used for eyebrows, and the tails can be sliced crossways to make eyes, noses or cheeks, or cut lengthways into strips and used for hair.

TIP

You can write a message to the birthday child, or write all the names of the guests. You could even play a game and the guests can make words from the letters you create.

WORD PLAY

1 Level cakes (page 333); secure cakes, cut-sides down, long sides together, on cake board with a little frosting. Tint remaining frosting blue; spread over top and sides of cake.

2 Cut licorice strap into lengths to fit around sides of cake. Cut 5 x 24cm (9½-inch) and 7 x 18cm (7¼-inch) long thin strips from licorice strap; using picture as a guide, position strips to create a grid.

3 Using a large sharp knife; carefully cut chocolate block into individual squares. Turn, top-side down. Using writing icing, write letters onto chocolate squares and position on and around word board.

4 Cut star shapes from sour strap; position on cake.

EQUIPMENT

- 30CM X 45CM (12-INCH X 18-INCH) RECTANGULAR CAKE BOARD (PAGE 332)

CAKE

- 1 X 450G (14½-OUNCE) PACKAGED DOUBLE UNFILLED SPONGE SLABS
- 1 X 453G (14½-OUNCE) TUB VANILLA FROSTING
- BLUE FOOD COLOURING

DECORATIONS

- 2 METRES (2 YARDS) BLACK LICORICE STRAP
- 220G (7-OUNCE) BLOCK WHITE CHOCOLATE
- BLACK WRITING ICING OR GEL
- 1 RED SOUR STRAP

ICE-CREAM SANDWICHES

EQUIPMENT

- 20CM X 30CM (8-INCH X 12-INCH) RECTANGULAR CAKE PAN
- 2 OVEN TRAYS
- 7.5CM (3-INCH) ROUND CUTTER

CAKE

- 2-LITRES (8-CUPS) VANILLA ICE-CREAM, SOFTENED
- 1 X 180G (5½-OUNCE) PACKET SMARTIES
- 1 X 450G (14½-OUNCE) PACKET READY-TO-BAKE M&M'S COOKIE DOUGH

1 Grease cake pan; line base and sides with baking paper, extending paper 5cm (2-inch) above sides (page 332).

2 Place ice-cream in a large bowl. Gently fold in Smarties. Spoon mixture into pan; smooth surface. Freeze 2 hours or overnight until firm.

3 Preheat oven to 180°C/350°F. Grease and line oven trays with baking paper.

4 Cut cookie dough into 16 x 1cm (½-inch) thick slices; place 2cm (¾-inch) apart on trays. Bake for 10 minutes or until golden brown. Cool on trays.

5 Cut eight rounds from ice-cream using cutter; sandwich each round between two cookies. Place on tray; freeze 30 minutes or overnight until firm.

TIPS Use strawberry or chocolate flavoured ice-cream instead of vanilla. Use any lollies you like in the ice-cream; if they are large, roughly chop them. Make this a rocky road ice-cream sandwich by adding chopped turkish delight, dark choc chips, peanuts and coconut. Make this cake the day before the party to allow ice-cream sandwiches time to become set.

TIP

We used 540g packets of vanilla cake mix which consist of a cake mix sachet and a frosting sachet (frosting not used).

RAINBOW CAKE

1 Preheat oven to 160°C/325°F. Grease cake pans. Line bases with baking paper.

2 Make cakes according to directions on packet. Measure 1⅓ cups of the mixture for each cake layer into eight separate bowls. Tint each cake layer (see tip).

3 Working with two coloured cake layers at a time, pour into prepared pans. Bake for 15 minutes or until cooked. Stand cakes in pan 5 minutes before turning, top-side up, onto a wire rack to cool. Wash, dry, grease and reline cake pans with baking paper. Repeat cooking remaining cake layers in batches.

4 Secure violet cake layer onto cake board with a little butter cream. Spoon butter cream into a large piping bag fitted with piping tube. Pipe a spiral layer of butter cream onto cake. Top with blue cake layer. Using picture as a guide continue layering cakes and butter cream. Decorate top of cake with assorted lollies.

TIP We used the following ratio of gel food colouring:

Violet layer
¼ teaspoon violet

Blue layer
½ teaspoon celestial blue

Aqua layer
⅛ teaspoon mint green +
¼ teaspoon celestial blue

Green layer
½ teaspoon mint green

Yellow layer
1½ teaspoon lemon yellow

Orange layer
½ teaspoon orange

Bright red layer
¼ teaspoon red +
¼ teaspoon orange

Deep red layer
1 teaspoon red +
1 drop violet

EQUIPMENT

- 2 X DEEP 20CM (8-INCH) ROUND CAKE PANS
- 30CM (12-INCH) ROUND CAKE BOARD (PAGE 332)
- 12MM (½-INCH) PLAIN PIPING TUBE

CAKE

- 3 X 540G (1 POUND) PACKETS VANILLA CAKE MIX
- VIOLET, CELESTIAL BLUE, MINT GREEN, LEMON YELLOW, ORANGE AND RED GEL FOOD COLOURING
- 6 QUANTITIES BUTTER CREAM (PAGE 327)

DECORATIONS

- ASSORTED LOLLIES

CAKE POPS

CAPPUCCINO POPS

- ½ CUP (75G) DARK CHOCOLATE MELTS
- METAL OR BAMBOO SKEWER
- 12 X 5G (¼-OUNCE) MINI CHOCOLATE CUPS
- 12 LOLLIPOP STICKS
- 12 WHITE MARSHMALLOWS
- COCOA POWDER, FOR DUSTING
- PAPER PIPING BAG (PAGE 336)

1 Melt chocolate (page 337).
2 Use skewer to pierce a hole through base of chocolate cups. Place a white marshmallow in centre of each cup.
3 Dip end of one lollipop stick into melted chocolate; push it through chocolate cup about halfway into marshmallow. Stand upright in a styrofoam block until set.
4 To make cup handles, spoon a little melted chocolate (re-melt if necessary) into piping bag; snip a small piece off corner. Pipe 12 small 'C' shapes onto a sheet of baking paper; stand until set. Attach handles to cups with a little melted chocolate. Dust tops of marshmallow with a little cocoa powder.

CHOC-MALLOW POPS

- 375G (12 OUNCES) WHITE CHOCOLATE MELTS
- 12 LOLLIPOP STICKS
- 12 PINK OR WHITE MARSHMALLOWS
- 12 CHOCOLATE FRECKLES

1 Melt chocolate (page 337).
2 Dip end of one lollipop stick into melted chocolate; push about halfway into a marshmallow. Repeat with remaining sticks and marshmallows. Stand upright in a styrofoam block until set.
3 Dip one marshmallow into melted chocolate (re-melt if necessary), rocking back and forth to coat (don't swirl pop or it will fall off). Allow excess chocolate to drip off. Stand upright in styrofoam block; top with a freckle. Repeat with remaining marshmallows and freckles. Re-melt chocolate if necessary. Stand pops until set.

TIP Decorate cake pops with small bows, if you like.

FLUTTER·BY POPS

- 150G (4½ OUNCES) DARK CHOCOLATE MELTS
- 100G (3 OUNCES) MINI MARSHMALLOWS
- ½ CUP (120G) JELLY RASPBERRIES, CHOPPED
- 12 MINI PAPER CASES (SEE TIP)
- 1 TABLESPOON BUTTERFLY SPRINKLES
- 12 LOLLIPOP STICKS

1 Melt chocolate (page 337).
2 Combine marshmallows, raspberries and three-quarters of the melted chocolate in a medium bowl; spoon a rounded teaspoonful of mixture into paper cases. Decorate with sprinkles. Refrigerate until set.
3 Dip end of one lollipop stick into melted chocolate (re-melt if necessary); push about halfway into marshmallow mixture. Stand upright in a styrofoam block until set.

TIPS Cut paper cases so they resemble grass, if you like. Pierce the bottom of the paper case with a metal skewer before inserting the lollipop stick.

MAGICAL MUSHROOMS POPS

- 375G (12 OUNCES) WHITE CHOCOLATE MELTS
- 12 LOLLIPOP STICKS
- 12 DOMED WHITE MARSHMALLOWS
- 36 MUSK LIFE SAVERS
- 6 STRAWBERRY SOUR STRAWS, SLICED THINLY

1 Melt chocolate (page 337).
2 Dip end of one lollipop stick into melted chocolate; push about halfway into a marshmallow. Repeat with remaining sticks and marshmallows. Stand upright in a styrofoam block until set.
3 Dip one marshmallow into melted chocolate (re-melt if necessary), rocking back and forth to coat (don't swirl pop or it will fall off). Allow excess chocolate to drip off. Using picture as a guide, thread three Life Savers onto bottom of pop, securing with a little melted chocolate. Stand upright in styrofoam block until set.
4 Secure sour straw slices to tops of mushrooms with a little melted chocolate.

GET THE PIE INTO THE OVEN

Follow the right path to the oven. Watch out for those dead ends!

A   B   C

DEAD END

DEAD END

WORD SEARCH

A	K	H	E	N	Z	W	M	W	E	W	E	B	P
O	L	B	F	V	D	D	G	S	G	A	M
T	I	Q	R	L	A	P	V	J	N	T	Z
C	M	E	O	Y	V	P	B	D	O	Y	A
T	P	T	S	U	G	A	R	K	P	A	F
L	E	A	T	B	F	B	N	F	S	K	L
O	U	L	I	W	R	U	C	I	D	B	O
L	H	O	N	G	K	T	A	L	L	Q	U
L	H	C	G	I	O	T	F	Q	X	L	R
I	V	O	S	G	G	E	Y	P	G	O	A
E	N	H	I	F	H	R	D	N	E	J	U
S	I	C	E	C	R	E	A	M	S	W	C

Find all the hidden words.

SUGAR   MILK   LOLLIES   VANILLA
FLOUR   BUTTER   FROSTING   CHOCOLATE
EGGS   ICE CREAM   PAN   SPONGE

Animals

TIPS

The sponge roll used here has a diameter of 10cm (4 inches) and a length of 16cm (6½ inches). Brush the sour strap with a little water to remove the sugar crystals.

PUPPY DOGS' TALES

1 Secure sponge roll to cake board with a little frosting. Using a small knife, cut one of the chocolate rollettes in half crossways; trim one half until it is slightly rounded, discard remaining half. Secure rollette to one end of sponge roll with a little frosting to form a nose for the dog.

2 Secure three of the chocolate rollettes to cake board with a little frosting. Trim remaining rollette into 1.5cm (¾-inch) cubes; secure to one end of each rollette with a little frosting to form noses for the puppies.

3 Spoon frosting into plastic lunch bag. Use kitchen scissors to snip a small opening in corner of bag. Pipe frosting in long lines, back and forth over bodies of dog and puppies, extending over back end and piping over noses.

4 Using a little frosting, secure blue M&Ms to white chocolate Melts; repeat with blue mini M&M's and Milkybar buttons. Secure chocolate Melts on dog for eyes and Milkybar buttons on puppies for eyes. Pipe remaining frosting around eyes to create a fringe.

5 Secure red M&M on dog for nose and red mini M&M's on puppies for noses. Use kitchen scissors to trim sour strap into a 4cm (1½-inch) long tongue for dog; attach tongue under nose.

EQUIPMENT

- 30CM X 40CM (12-INCH X 16-INCH) RECTANGULAR CAKE BOARD (PAGE 332)
- LARGE PLASTIC LUNCH BAG OR PIPING BAG

CAKE

- 1 X 500G (1-POUND) PACKET DOUBLE CHOCOLATE SPONGE ROLL
- 2 X 453G (14½-OUNCE) TUBS DARK CHOCOLATE FROSTING
- 5 CHOCOLATE ROLLETTES

DECORATIONS

- 2 BLUE M&M'S
- 2 WHITE CHOCOLATE MELTS
- 6 BLUE MINI M&M'S
- 6 MILKYBAR BUTTONS
- 1 RED M&M
- 3 RED MINI M&M'S
- 1 RED SOUR STRAP

RAINBOW FISH

1 Secure one of the cakes to cake board with a little frosting. Using picture as a guide, cut tail and fin shapes from remaining cake; secure to cake with a little frosting.

2 Tint frosting blue; spread over top and sides of cake.

3 Using oiled kitchen scissors, cut jubes in half crossways; using picture as a guide, decorate fish with jubes as scales. Trim sour straps and use to make a tail fin. Position marshmallow half, jube half and Tic Tac half on cake for an eye; secure with a little frosting. Position jelly beans for mouth.

EQUIPMENT

- 20 X 30CM (8-INCH X 12-INCH) RECTANGULAR CAKE BOARD (PAGE 332)

CAKE

- 2 X 600G (1¼-POUND) PACKETS WHITE CHOCOLATE MUD CAKE
- 1 X 453G (14½-OUNCE) TUB VANILLA FROSTING
- BLUE FOOD COLOURING

DECORATIONS

- 1 X 300G (9½-OUNCE) PACKET JUBES
- 4 RAINBOW SOUR STRAPS
- 1 LARGE WHITE MARSHMALLOW, HALVED CROSSWAYS
- 1 ROUND BLACK JUBE, HALVED CROSSWAYS
- 1 WHITE TIC TAC, HALVED CROSSWAYS
- 2 RED JELLY BEANS

TIPS

You can use jelly beans or rainbow straps to decorate the fish. If using butter cream instead of vanilla frosting, you will need one quantity of butter cream (page 327).

TIPS
You need 1 sponge cake round and 2 sponge cake slabs for this recipe. If you don't have an 11cm (4½-inch) round cutter, simply use a saucer or bowl instead.

CIRCUS ELLE-PHANT

1 Secure round cake to cake board with a little frosting. Using 11cm cutter, cut two rounds from one of the slab cakes. Use a knife to shape a 1cm (½-inch) curve into each round; secure to round cake with a little frosting to form ears. Use a sharp knife to cut remaining slab cake into a 15cm x 7cm (6-inch x 2¾-inch) rectangle; secure to round cake with a little frosting to form trunk. Trim trunk to curve slightly.

2 Tint frosting grey using black colouring. Spread over top and sides of cake. Use bamboo skewer to make trunk creases. Position bananas to form tusks.

3 Knead ready-made icing on a surface dusted with a little icing sugar until icing loses its stickiness. Divide icing into three balls; tint one ball pink and one ball blue; leave remaining ball white. Roll pink icing out on a surface dusted with a little icing sugar until 3mm (⅛-inch) thick (page 334). Using 8cm cutter, cut two rounds from icing. Trim 1cm (½-inch) off each round. Position icing on each ear, using picture as a guide.

4 Roll white icing on a surface dusted with a little icing sugar until 3mm (⅛-inch) thick. Using 4cm cutter, cut two rounds from icing. Roll blue icing on a surface dusted with a little icing sugar until 3mm (⅛-inch) thick. Using 3cm cutter, cut two rounds from icing. Secure blue icing to white icing with a little water. Position on cake to form eyes.

5 Secure jubes to blue icing. Roll a little of the remaining white icing into small balls; secure to jubes with a little water to form pupils.

EQUIPMENT

- 25CM X 35CM (10-INCH X 14-INCH) RECTANGULAR CAKE BOARD (PAGE 332)
- 11CM (4½-INCH), 8CM (3¼-INCH), 4CM (1½-INCH) AND 3CM (1¼-INCH) ROUND CUTTERS
- 1 BAMBOO SKEWER

CAKE

- ½ X 460G (14½-OUNCE) PACKAGED DOUBLE UNFILLED SPONGE CAKE ROUNDS
- 1 X 453G (14½-OUNCE) TUB VANILLA FROSTING
- 1 X 450G (14½-OUNCE) PACKAGED DOUBLE UNFILLED SPONGE SLABS
- BLACK, PINK AND BLUE FOOD COLOURING
- 50G (1½ OUNCES) READY-MADE WHITE ICING (PAGE 327)
- PURE ICING (CONFECTIONERS') SUGAR, FOR DUSTING

DECORATIONS

- 2 YELLOW BANANA LOLLIES
- 1 ROUND BLACK JUBE, HALVED

NEVER SMILE AT A
CROCODILE

1 Make jelly according to directions on packet. Pour into tray; refrigerate 1 hour or until set.

2 Position cakes, side-by-side, short ends together. Using a small serrated knife, trim cakes into a crocodile shape. Use cake off-cuts to make legs. Position cakes on jelly.

3 Tint frosting green; carefully spread frosting all over top and sides of cake.

4 Using picture as a guide, position spearmint leaves, cut-side up, over crocodile's body.

5 Using kitchen scissors, cut small wedges from teeth to create pointy teeth; position around mouth. Secure M&M's on end of nose for nostrils. Secure marshmallow on top of head for eyes, then attach licorice with a little frosting for pupils.

6 Cut tops from milk bottles; cut each milk bottle into three lengthways. Position on legs as claws.

TIPS You will need 3 sponge slabs for this recipe. If you don't like spearmint leaves, use green racing car lollies or green jubes for scales as an alternative. If using butter cream instead of vanilla frosting, you will need 2 quantities of butter cream (page 327).

EQUIPMENT
- 35CM X 45CM (14-INCH X 18-INCH) LARGE SHALLOW PLASTIC TRAY

CAKE
- 1 X 85G (3-OUNCE) PACKET BLUEBERRY JELLY
- 1½ X 450G (14½-OUNCE) PACKAGED DOUBLE UNFILLED SPONGE SLABS
- 2 X 453G (14½-OUNCE) TUBS VANILLA FROSTING
- GREEN FOOD COLOURING

DECORATIONS
- 3 X 300G (9½-OUNCE) PACKETS SPEARMINT LEAVES, HALVED HORIZONTALLY
- 6 JELLY TEETH
- 2 BROWN M&M'S
- 1 WHITE MARSHMALLOW, HALVED CROSSWAYS
- 1CM (½-INCH) PIECE LICORICE TWIST, HALVED CROSSWAYS
- 4 WHITE MILK BOTTLES

LIFE IN A FISH BOWL

1 Position jubes in base of glass bowl. Make one packet of the jelly following packet directions; tint pale blue. Pour enough jelly into glass bowl to just cover jubes (you don't want them to float). Refrigerate until jelly is set.

2 To make fish, place two apricot halves together; place on a small oven tray. Cut sour strap into fin shapes; push in between apricot halves to secure. Gently push a choc Bit into apricot for an eye. Repeat with remaining apricots, sour strap and choc Bits; freeze 1 hour or until firm.

3 Tie bunches of rainbow laces together, knotting at one end. Push laces into jelly, making sure they are firmly in place. Make remaining jelly following packet directions; tint pale blue. Pour jelly into bowl (sour straps may float up, but should be anchored at the base to form seaweed). Refrigerate 1 hour or until nearly set.

4 When jelly is almost set, push fish into jelly with eye up against glass. Refrigerate until jelly is completely set. Sprinkle top of jelly with hundreds & thousands as fish food.

TIPS Start making this jelly cake 6 hours ahead of the party to allow the jelly to set between stages. We used create-a-jelly (available from larger supermarkets), which are clear jelly crystals that you add your own flavours and colours to, this way you can control the depth of colour. You can use blue or green jelly crystals, if you like, but it will be darker in colour and you may not be able to see the details in the fish bowl as well.

EQUIPMENT
- 1-LITRE (4-CUP) GLASS BOWL

CAKE
- 4 X 85G (3-OUNCE) PACKETS CREATE-A-JELLY CRYSTALS
- BLUE FOOD COLOURING

DECORATIONS
- 30 YELLOW JUBES
- 4 DRAINED CANNED APRICOT HALVES
- 2 RED SOUR STRAPS
- 2 DARK CHOCOLATE BITS
- 4 GREEN BOOTLACES
- ¼ TEASPOON HUNDREDS & THOUSANDS

BABY BEAR

EQUIPMENT

- 31CM X 34CM (12½-INCH X 13½-INCH) TEDDY BEAR CAKE PAN
- 38CM X 47CM (15¼-INCH X 18¾-INCH) RECTANGULAR CAKE BOARD (PAGE 332)

CAKE

- 2 X 340G (11-OUNCE) PACKETS BUTTER CAKE MIX
- 1 QUANTITY BUTTER CREAM (PAGE 327)
- 1 TABLESPOON COCOA POWDER
- BROWN FOOD COLOURING

DECORATIONS

- 2 BLUE SMARTIES
- 2 MILKYBAR BUTTONS
- 1 PEACHES & CREAM LOLLY
- 1 ORANGE JELLY SNAKE
- ORANGE SPRINKLES
- 12 CARAMEL MILK BOTTLES
- 4 STRAWBERRY MILK BOTTLES
- 7 STRAWBERRIES & CREAM LOLLIES

1 Preheat oven to 180°C/350°F. Grease cake pan, dust lightly with flour; shake off excess (page 332).

2 Make cakes according to directions on packets. Spread mixture into pan; bake about 45 minutes. Stand cake in pan 5 minutes before turning, top-side up, onto wire rack to cool.

3 Trim bottom of cake so cake lies flat. Secure cake on cake board with a little butter cream.

4 Stir sifted cocoa into butter cream, tint with brown colouring. Spread brown butter cream all over cake.

5 Using a little of the butter cream, secure Smarties onto Milkybar buttons and position on face for eyes. Position peaches & cream as nose. Trim and cut snake to resemble mouth, position on cake. Sprinkle cheeks with sprinkles.

6 Cut caramel milk bottles in half lengthways; using picture as a guide, position on bear's belly. Position strawberry milk bottles to form a bow tie.

7 Cut one strawberries & cream in half crossways, position on cake in ears. Trim tops from four strawberries & cream; trim one end off each and join two ends together, position in centre of bottom paws. Position remaining strawberries & cream, up-side down, in centre of upper paws.

TIP
Peaches & cream and
strawberries & cream can
be found in packets
of party mx.

TIP
Use iced chocolate doughnuts as nests instead of cinnamon doughnuts.

FREE-RANGE CHICKENS

1 Tint frosting with yellow colouring. Tint coconut yellow (page 336).

2 Spread frosting over mini doughnuts; roll in coconut to coat. Stand mini doughnuts in centre of cinnamon doughnuts.

3 Position blue M&M's on marshmallow halves with a little frosting; pipe black dots for pupils with decorating gel, secure on coconut for eyes. Position orange M&M's to form beaks.

CAKE

- ½ X 453G (14½-OUNCE) TUB VANILLA FROSTING
- YELLOW FOOD COLOURING
- 6 MINI DOUGHNUTS
- 6 CINNAMON DOUGHNUTS

DECORATIONS

- 1 CUP (70G) MOIST COCONUT FLAKES
- 12 BLUE MINI M&M'S
- 6 MINI WHITE MARSHMALLOWS, HALVED
- BLACK DECORATING GEL
- 12 ORANGE MINI M&M'S

BEAUTIFUL BUTTERFLY

EQUIPMENT

- TWO 18CM (7¼-INCH) HEART-SHAPED CAKE PANS
- 12-HOLE (⅓-CUP/80ML) STANDARD MUFFIN PAN
- 4 YELLOW PAPER MUFFIN CASES
- 40CM X 55CM (16-INCH X 22-INCH) RECTANGULAR CAKE BOARD (PAGE 332)

CAKE

- 2 X 340G (11-OUNCE) PACKETS BUTTER CAKE MIX
- 2 QUANTITIES BUTTER CREAM (PAGE 327)
- GREEN AND PINK FOOD COLOURINGS

DECORATIONS

- 3 X 190G (6-OUNCE) PACKETS JELLY BEANS
- 2 GREEN SMARTIES
- 2 X 30CM (12-INCH) THIN YELLOW CHENILLE STICKS (PIPE CLEANERS)

1 Preheat oven to 180°C/350°F. Grease pans; line bases with baking paper. Line 4 holes of muffin pan with paper cases.

2 Make cakes according to directions on packets. Drop ¼-cups of mixture into each paper case; bake about 20 minutes. Divide remaining mixture between pans; bake about 35 minutes. Stand cakes in pans 5 minutes before turning, top-side up, onto wire racks to cool.

3 Using a serrated knife, level tops of heart cakes so they are same height. Turn heart cakes cut-side down; secure muffins and heart cakes on cake board with a little butter cream to form butterfly, as pictured.

4 Place a quarter of the butter cream into a small bowl; tint pale green. Tint remaining butter cream pale pink. Spread muffins with green icing; spread heart cakes with pink icing.

5 Divide jelly beans into same colours. Using picture as a guide; decorate wings and body of butterfly with jelly beans. Position Smarties for eyes. Twist chenille sticks to resemble antennae; position on butterfly's head.

TIP

Macaroons are available from specialty bakery shops and select supermarkets. If you can't find them, any small round filled biscuit will do. Try mini Oreos or mini Wagon Wheels.

OLIVIA LONGNECK

1 Secure cake to cake board with a little frosting. Spread frosting over top and side of cake.

2 Using picture as a guide, build emu's neck with Venetian biscuits, securing together with a little frosting.

3 Position muffin at top of neck for head; secure with a little frosting. Spread top and side with frosting.

4 Using picture as a guide, decorate head and body with coconut.

5 Cut wafer into two triangles; position on head for beak. Position marshmallow on head for eye, top with jube and Tic Tac for pupil; secure with a little frosting.

6 Using picture as a guide, build emu's leg with macaroons, attaching together with a little frosting. Position three banana halves for claws.

7 Position finger biscuits on cake board at back of emu's body to resemble tail feathers.

EQUIPMENT

- 30CM X 50CM (12-INCH X 20-INCH) RECTANGULAR CAKE BOARD (PAGE 332)

CAKE

- 1 X 600G (1¼-POUND) PACKET ROUND CHOCOLATE MUD CAKE
- 1 X 453G (14½-OUNCE) TUB DARK CHOCOLATE FROSTING
- 1 X 115G (3½ OUNCES) LARGE CHOCOLATE MUFFIN

DECORATIONS

- 2 X 200G (6½-OUNCE) PACKETS VENETIAN BISCUITS
- ½ CUP (50G) SHREDDED COCONUT
- 1 ICE-CREAM WAFER
- ½ WHITE MARSHMALLOW
- ½ ROUND BLACK JUBE
- 1 MINT TIC TAC
- 8 YELLOW MACAROONS (SEE TIPS)
- 2 YELLOW BANANA LOLLIES, HALVED LENGTHWAYS
- 15 CHOCOLATE FINGER BISCUITS

WILBUR
THE WOMBAT

EQUIPMENT

- 20CM X 30CM (8-INCH X 12-INCH) RECTANGULAR CAKE BOARD (PAGE 332)

CAKE

- 1 X 480G (15½-OUNCE) PACKET DOUBLE CHOCOLATE LOAF CAKE
- 1 X 453G (14½-OUNCE) TUB DARK CHOCOLATE FROSTING

DECORATIONS

- 2 TEASPOONS COCOA POWDER
- 1 WHITE MARSHMALLOW, HALVED CROSSWAYS
- 1 ROUND BLACK JUBE, HALVED CROSSWAYS
- 1 WHITE TIC TAC, HALVED CROSSWAYS
- 1 CHOCOLATE CLINKER
- 4 MILK CHOCOLATE MELTS

1 Using a small serrated knife, trim cake to form a rounded shape for wombat; reserve cake scraps. Secure cake to cake board with a little frosting.

2 Place reserved cake scraps and 2 tablespoons of the frosting in a small bowl; mash with a fork until combined. Using picture as a guide, make four leg shapes from cake mixture; secure to cake with a little frosting. Spread top and sides of cake with frosting. Drag a fork down frosting to get a furry look. Sprinkle with sifted cocoa.

3 Using picture as a guide, position marshmallow halves, jube halves and Tic Tac halves for eyes, securing with a little frosting. Position Clinker for nose. Cut two chocolate Melts in half; place on wombat's head for ears. Cut remaining chocolate Melts into long slivers, position on end of wombat's legs as claws.

TIP
If using butter cream instead of chocolate frosting, you will need one quantity of chocolate butter cream (page 327).

TIP

If using butter cream instead of vanilla frosting, you will need one quantity of butter cream (page 327).

HERE KITTY KITTY

1 Secure cake to cake board with a little frosting. Cut muffin into quarters. Trim round side of two muffin pieces into triangles; secure to cake with a little frosting to form ears. Discard remaining muffin.

2 Tint frosting orange. Spread over top and sides of cake and muffin.

3 Knead ready-made icing on a surface dusted with a little sifted icing sugar until icing loses its stickiness. Tint half the icing blue.

4 Roll white icing on a surface dusted with a little icing sugar until 3mm (⅛-inch) thick (page 334). Using 4cm cutter, cut two rounds from icing. Roll blue icing on a surface dusted with a little icing sugar until 3mm (⅛-inch) thick. Using 1cm cutter, cut two rounds from icing. Secure blue rounds to white rounds with a little water to form eyes; position on cake.

Cut two small strips of licorice; secure to eyes with a little water, for pupils.

5 Secure marshmallow on centre of cake for nose. Cut remaining licorice into two thin strips; position on cake to form mouth. Shape a 4cm (1½-inch) piece of sour strap into a tongue shape, secure to cake. Cut 6 x 3mm (⅛-inch) thin strips from yellow part of roll up; position on cake to form whiskers.

6 Discard red section from strawberries & cream; position white part as ears, as pictured. Decorate cake with a bow, if you like.

EQUIPMENT

- 30CM (12-INCH) ROUND CAKE BOARD (PAGE 332)
- 4CM (1½-INCH) AND 1CM (½-INCH) ROUND CUTTERS

CAKE

- 1 X 600G (1¼-POUND) PACKET ROUND CHOCOLATE MUD CAKE
- ½ X 453G (14½-OUNCE) TUB VANILLA FROSTING
- 1 X 115G (3½ OUNCES) LARGE BLUEBERRY MUFFIN
- ORANGE AND BLUE FOOD COLOURING
- 20G (¾ OUNCE) READY-MADE WHITE ICING (PAGE 327)
- PURE ICING (CONFECTIONERS') SUGAR, FOR DUSTING

DECORATIONS

- 20CM (8-INCH) PIECE BLACK LICORICE STRAP
- 1 PINK MARSHMALLOW, HALVED CROSSWAYS
- 1 RED SOUR STRAP
- 1 FRUIT SALAD ROLL UP
- 2 STRAWBERRIES & CREAM LOLLIES

MONKEY BUSINESS

EQUIPMENT

- 30CM (12-INCH) ROUND CAKE BOARD (PAGE 332)
- DISPOSABLE PLASTIC PIPING BAG OR PLASTIC LUNCH BAG

CAKE

- 1 X 600G (1¼-POUND) PACKET ROUND CHOCOLATE MUD CAKE
- ½ X 453G (14½-OUNCE) TUB DARK CHOCOLATE FROSTING
- 2 X 115G (3½ OUNCES) LARGE BLUEBERRY MUFFINS
- ½ X 453G (14½-OUNCE) TUB VANILLA FROSTING

DECORATIONS

- 2 ORANGE SMARTIES
- 10CM (4-INCH) PIECE BLACK LICORICE STRAP
- 2 LARGE CHOCOLATE COINS, UNWRAPPED
- 1 WHITE MARSHMALLOW, HALVED CROSSWAYS
- 2 BLUE SMARTIES
- 2 ICE-CREAM WAFERS

1 Secure cake to cake board with a little frosting. Cut 2cm (¾-inch) from base of muffins; reserve one of the off-cuts. Trim 2cm (¾-inch) lengthways off each muffin. Secure muffins to cake, with a little frosting to form ears. Spread top and sides of cake and muffins with chocolate frosting.

2 Position reserved muffin off-cut on cake for nose. Place vanilla frosting in piping bag; snip a medium opening in one corner. Using picture as a guide, pipe over nose and pipe two large circles on cake to form eyes; smooth frosting. Position orange Smarties and licorice on muffin to form nose and mouth.

3 Top eyes with chocolate coins; secure marshmallow halves and blue Smarties to coins with a little frosting.

4 Trim wafers, using picture as a guide; position wafers on ears.

TIPS Add licorice eyelashes to make Millie, if you like; just cut into a piece of black licorice strap to make the lashes. If using butter cream instead of frostings, you need one quantity of butter cream (page 327). Add 1½ tablespoons sifted cocoa to half the mixture to make chocolate butter cream.

JIMMY JELLYFISH

1 Preheat oven to 180°C/350°F. Grease baking dish; line base and sides with baking paper, extending paper 5cm (2-inch) above sides.

2 Make cakes according to directions on packets. Spread mixture into dish; bake about 1 hour. Stand cake in dish 20 minutes before turning, top-side up, onto a wire rack to cool.

3 Dissolve jelly in a large heatproof bowl using 3 cups boiling water and 2½ cups cold water. Refrigerate until set.

4 Using a serrated knife, level cake top. Turn cake cut-side down. Using picture as a guide, cut jellyfish shape from cake. Place in tray.

5 Tint butter cream mauve. Spread butter cream over top and sides of cake.

6 Position chocolate Melts on cake for eyes; secure Smarties to top of melts with a little butter cream.

7 Using picture as a guide, decorate cake with nerds.

8 Using whisk, break up jelly; spoon carefully into tray around cake.

9 Cut nerds ropes in half; position below cake as tentacles. Pinch milk bottles to form a fish shape; position in jelly.

TIP Refrigerate cake if weather is hot.

EQUIPMENT

- DEEP 26CM X 33CM (10½-INCH X 13¼-INCH) BAKING DISH
- 35CM X 45CM (14-INCH X 18-INCH) LARGE SHALLOW PLASTIC TRAY

CAKE

- 3 X 340G (11-OUNCE) PACKETS BUTTER CAKE MIX
- 4 X 85G (3-OUNCE) PACKETS BLUE JELLY CRYSTALS
- 1 QUANTITY BUTTER CREAM (PAGE 327)
- MAUVE FOOD COLOURING

DECORATIONS

- 2 WHITE CHOCOLATE MELTS
- 2 BLUE SMARTIES
- 1 TABLESPOON GRAPE NERDS
- 4 X 25G (¾-OUNCE) PACKETS NERDS ROPE
- 7 WHITE MILK BOTTLES

QUIET AS A
MOUSE

EQUIPMENT

- 30CM (12-INCH) ROUND
  CAKE BOARD (PAGE 332)
- 1 SMALL PLASTIC ZIPTOP BAG

CAKE

- 1 X 450G (14½-OUNCE) PACKET
  DOUBLE ROUND UNFILLED
  SPONGE CAKE
- 1 X 453G (14½-OUNCE) TUB
  VANILLA FROSTING
- BLACK FOOD COLOURING

DECORATIONS

- 2 LARGE DOMED
  PINK MARSHMALLOWS,
  HALVED HORIZONTALLY
- 1 WHITE MARSHMALLOW,
  HALVED HORIZONTALLY
- 1 BLACK ROUND JUBE
- 1 WHITE TIC TAC
- 1 PINK MUSK STICK
- 1 SUGAR-FREE DOUBLE D
  PINK LOLLY

1 Level cake tops (page 333). Spread one cake with a little frosting; top with remaining cake. Using picture as a guide, trim cake into a heart shape, removing as little of cake as possible. Secure cake to cake board using a little frosting.

2 Reserve ⅓ cup of the frosting; tint remaining frosting grey. Spread grey frosting all over cake. Spoon reserved frosting into ziptop bag, snip one corner, carefully pipe a heart-shaped face in centre of cake, fill with remaining white frosting, smooth with a spatula.

3 Flatten each bottom half of pink marshmallows with palm of your hand and position on cake for ears, top with white marshmallow halves. Cut jube in half horizontally; position cut-side up on face for eyes. Cut Tic Tac in half crossways; position on top of eyes for pupils. Cut musk stick in half crossways then slice each half into long thin strips, position on cake as whiskers. Position double D lolly for nose.

TIP
Teeth and milk bottles can be found in packets of party mix.

OLIVER THE LION

1 Preheat oven to 180°C/350°F. Grease cake pan; line base with baking paper. Grease 20 holes of the friand pans.

2 Make cakes according to directions on packets. Drop 2½ level tablespoons of the mixture into each friand hole; bake about 20 minutes. Spread remaining mixture into cake pan; bake about 50 minutes. Stand cakes in pans 5 minutes before turning, top-side up, onto wire racks to cool.

3 Using a serrated knife, level top of cake; turn cake cut-side down. Secure cake on cake board with a little butter cream.

4 Tint butter cream yellow. Spread butter cream over top and side of all cakes and over top of biscuits; sprinkle biscuits with sprinkles.

5 Using picture as a guide, position friands around cake. Position biscuits on round cake to make ears, nose and cheeks.

6 Reserve six chocolate Melts. Melt remaining white chocolate (page 337), pour into piping bag; snip a small opening from tip. Pipe about 60 fans of chocolate onto baking-paper-lined trays. Refrigerate 5 minutes or until set.

7 Using picture as a guide, position chocolate fans overlapping to make mane.

8 Trim teeth and milk bottles; position for lion's mouth. Position lollipop as tongue. Position reserved chocolate Melts on cake for eyes and attach jubes to chocolate Melts using a little butter cream. Trim an edge off freckles; position on ears.

9 Shape a 3cm (1¼-inch) piece of the licorice into a nose shape; position on cake. Cut six thin strips of the licorice; position on cake as whiskers.

EQUIPMENT

- DEEP 30CM (12-INCH) ROUND CAKE PAN
- 3 X 9-HOLE (½-CUP/125ML) FRIAND PANS
- 50CM (20-INCH) ROUND CAKE BOARD (PAGE 332)
- PAPER PIPING BAG (PAGE 336)

CAKE

- 5 X 340G (11-OUNCE) PACKETS BUTTER CAKE MIX
- 1½ QUANTITIES BUTTER CREAM (PAGE 327)
- BUTTERCUP YELLOW FOOD COLOURING

DECORATIONS

- 6 MILK ARROWROOT BISCUITS
- 2 TABLESPOONS YELLOW SPRINKLES
- 375G (12 OUNCES) WHITE CHOCOLATE MELTS
- 1 JELLY TEETH
- 2 WHITE MILK BOTTLES
- 1 RED LOLLIPOP
- 2 GREEN JUBES
- 2 CHOCOLATE FRECKLES
- 20CM (8-INCH) PIECE BLACK LICORICE STRAP

FRANKFURT THE SAUSAGE DOG

EQUIPMENT

- 30CM X 45CM (12-INCH X 18-INCH) RECTANGULAR CAKE BOARD (PAGE 332)
- WOODEN TOOTHPICKS
- WOODEN SKEWERS

CAKE

- 3 X CHOCOLATE ROLLETTES
- 1 X 400G (12½-OUNCE) PACKET CHOCOLATE SPONGE ROLL
- 1 X 453G (14½-OUNCE) TUB CHOCOLATE FROSTING
- 1 X 125G (4-OUNCE) DOUBLE CHOCOLATE-CHIP MUFFIN

DECORATIONS

- 1 X 5CM (2-INCH) PIECE SMOOTH LICORICE
- 2 RED SOUR STRAPS
- 1 WHITE MARSHMALLOW
- 1 BLACK JELLY BEAN
- 6 WHITE TIC TACS
- 2 CHOCOLATE MONTE BISCUITS
- 1 JELLY SWEETHEART
- 1 YELLOW BOOTLACE

1 Cut two of the rollettes in half. Using picture as a guide, position sponge roll (body) on top of halved rollettes (legs) on cake board, securing with a little frosting and toothpicks, if needed.

2 Position muffin on its side on top of one end of sponge roll to make head (flat end at front); secure with skewers, trimming if necessary. Trim 1cm (½ inch) from remaining rollette and discard; secure remaining rollette to muffin for snout with a little frosting and toothpicks. Use a small serrated knife to trim back end of dog into a rounded shape.

3 Spread frosting all over cake. Using a small knife, press lightly into frosting to make short fur.

4 Cut a small slice from licorice, shape into a triangle and position for nose. Cut a 2cm (¾-inch) thin piece of sour strap; split halfway down length; position as an upside-down 'Y' shape under nose.

5 Cut marshmallow in half; position, cut-side up, for eyes. Cut jelly bean in half, secure on top of marshmallow halves. Cut Tic Tacs in half; position for claws.

6 Trim end of remaining licorice into a point; push into cake to make tail. Attach biscuits for ears, securing with a little frosting.

7 To make collar, trim sour strap to fit around dog's neck. Pierce heart with a skewer, push through a piece of bootlace and position around collar for tag. Secure collar around neck with a little frosting and a toothpick, if needed.

TIP We used ⅔ cup brown mini M&M's and a small bowl for kibble.

SAMMY: SHARK SECURITY

1 Secure two of the cakes, long sides together, with a little frosting; spread top with a little frosting and top with remaining cakes. Cut out shark body and tail fin using templates (page 339).

2 Tint frosting grey with a little black colouring. Secure shark to cake board with a little frosting. Spread frosting all over cake.

3 Position mentos on cake for eye, securing with a little frosting. Secure jube half to top of mentos; cut a small sliver of the marshmallow and position on jube.

4 Cut licorice into 3 long thin strips; position on cake for gills.

5 Using kitchen scissors, trim white sections of teeth into sharp points. Position teeth on cake, trimming to fit. Trim pineapple lollies into fish shapes. Cut pieces of licorice into tiny cubes; position on pineapple lollies for fish eyes.

TIPS You can make fish eyes with black writing icing, if you prefer. We used different-sized marshmallows for the bubbles on the cake board.

EQUIPMENT
- 35CM X 50CM (14-INCH X 20-INCH) RECTANGULAR CAKE BOARD (PAGE 332)

CAKE
- 2 X 450G (14½-OUNCE) PACKETS DOUBLE UNFILLED SPONGE SLABS
- 1 X 453G (14½-OUNCE) TUB VANILLA FROSTING
- BLACK FOOD COLOURING

DECORATIONS
- 1 WHITE MENTOS
- 1 BLACK ROUND JUBE, HALVED
- 1 MINI WHITE MARSHMALLOW
- 5CM (2-INCH) PIECE LICORICE STRAP
- 2 JELLY TEETH
- 9 PINEAPPLE LOLLIES

PEACOCK POMP
AND PAGEANTRY

EQUIPMENT

- 30CM X 40XM (12-INCH X 16-INCH) RECTANGULAR CAKE BOARD (PAGE 332)
- 13 X 16CM (6½-INCH) WOODEN SKEWERS

CAKE

- 1 X 450G (14½-OUNCE) PACKET DOUBLE UNFILLED SPONGE SLABS
- 1 X 453G (14½-OUNCE) TUB VANILLA FROSTING
- BLUE FOOD COLOURING

DECORATIONS

- 25 JUBES
- 26 FRUIT JELLY WEDGES
- 13 JELLY RASPBERRIES
- 13 RAINBOW SOUR STRAPS
- 14 FRUIT RINGS
- 14 BOILED LOLLIES
- 7 BLACK JELLY BEANS, HALVED
- 1 ICE-CREAM WAFER, TRIMMED INTO A TRIANGLE SHAPE
- 2CM (¾-INCH) PIECE LICORICE STRAP

1 Place cakes together, long sides touching; secure with a little frosting. Cut out peacock shape using template (page 338). Secure peacock to cake board with a little frosting.

2 Tint frosting blue. Spread frosting all over cake, adding a little texture for feathers using tip of a palette knife.

3 Using picture as a guide, thread skewers with lollies to make peacock's tail, ending with a fruit ring topped with a boiled lolly and jelly bean half.

4 Cut wafer into a 2cm (¾-inch) triangle; position for beak. Cut remaining fruit ring in half; place at bottom of peacock for feet. Shape licorice strap into an eye shape; top with remaining boiled lolly and remaining jelly bean half.

TIPS Make as many lolly skewers as there are children at the party. If the skewers don't all fit around the cake have them standing in a wide mouth glass or vase. Remove the skewers from cake before serving.

WHO'S A CUTE DOGGY THEN?

1 Divide frosting into three small bowls. Tint one bowl pale grey, one pale brown and leave remaining bowl plain.

2 Discard paper cases from mini muffins; spread each frosting over four mini muffins. Secure mini muffins, sideways, on top of muffins, with a little frosting.

3 Spread grey frosting all over four cakes. Cut licorice strap into 3 x 5cm (2-inch) slices; using picture as a guide, trim to resemble ears and nose. Halve one jelly bean for eyes, and halve one jelly bean lengthways for nose; position on cake. Trim sour strap into a 1.5cm (½-inch) piece for tongue; position on cake. Repeat with remaining grey cakes.

4 Spread brown frosting all over four cakes. Using picture as a guide, position a milk chocolate melt for nose; secure a thin slice of soft licorice onto melt with a little frosting. Cut marshmallows in half; attach one brown M&M to one half; position on cake for eye. Attach another brown M&M onto face for eye. Using picture as a guide, trim licorice strap into 2 x 3cm (1¼-inch) pieces for ears; position on cake. Repeat with remaining brown cakes.

5 Place plain frosting into piping bag fitted with fluted tube. Pipe all over remaining four cakes to add texture. Using picture as a guide, position white chocolate Melts to form ears and nose. Trim a small piece of licorice strap into a triangle for nose. Cut 1 jelly bean in half and position for eyes. Cut pink section of licorice allsort into triangles and position on top of cake for bow. Cut red sour strap into thirds lengthways, place around neck for collar; position yellow MM for tag. Repeat with remaining plain cakes.

EQUIPMENT

- 1 DISPOSABLE PIPING BAG
- 1.5CM (¾-INCH) FLUTED TUBE

CAKE

- 1 X 453G (14½-OUNCE) TUB VANILLA FROSTING
- BLACK AND BROWN FOOD COLOURINGS
- 12 DOUBLE CHOCOLATE-CHIP MINI MUFFINS
- 12 DOUBLE CHOCOLATE-CHIP MUFFINS

DECORATIONS

- 1M (1 YARD) BLACK LICORICE STRAP
- 12 BLACK JELLY BEANS
- 5 RED SOUR STRAPS
- 4 MILK CHOCOLATE MELTS
- 1 SMALL PIECE ROUND SOFT-EATING LICORICE
- 2 WHITE MARSHMALLOWS
- 8 BROWN MINI M&MS
- 12 WHITE CHOCOLATE MELTS
- 4 PINK LICORICE ALLSORTS
- 4 YELLOW MINI M&MS

FLAMENCO FLAMINGO

EQUIPMENT
- 30CM X 40CM (12-INCH X 16-INCH) RECTANGULAR CAKE BOARD (PAGE 332)

CAKE
- 2 X 450G (14½-OUNCE) PACKETS DOUBLE UNFILLED SPONGE SLABS
- 1 X 453G (14½-OUNCE) TUB VANILLA FROSTING
- PINK FOOD COLOURING

DECORATIONS
- 375G (12 OUNCE) STRAWBERRIES, SLICED
- 8 EXTREME RED SOUR STRAPS
- 50G (1½-OUNCE) MILK CHOCOLATE MELTS
- 2 BANANA LOLLIES
- 1 WHITE MARSHMALLOW, HALVED
- 1 SUGAR-FREE DOUBLE D PINK LOLLY
- 1 SOFT BLACK LICORICE, SLICED THINLY
- 11 PINK MUSK STICKS

1 Using templates as a guide (page 338), cut one of the sandwiched sponge cakes into flamingo's body. Secure to cake board with a little frosting. Cut flamingo's head and neck from remaining sandwiched sponge cake. Secure in position with a little frosting.

2 Tint frosting pink. Spread frosting over top and sides of cake. Using picture as a guide, decorate body with sliced strawberries.

3 Cut sour straps into long pieces, position on cake for wing.

4 Melt the chocolate (page 337). Dip one end of each banana into melted chocolate; place on baking paper to set. Position bananas on head for beak. Position marshmallow, double D lolly and licorice for eye and musk sticks for legs.

TIP Position strawberry slices on the flamingo shortly before serving.

SEA CREATURES

MYRTLE THE TURTLE

- ½ X 453G (14½-OUNCE) TUB DARK CHOCOLATE FROSTING
- 3 X 460G (14½-OUNCE) PACKETS MUFFINS
- 24 EACH GREEN AND PURPLE SOFT SQUARE OR DIAMOND JUBES, HALVED CROSSWAYS
- 30 SPEARMINT LEAVES, HALVED CROSSWAYS
- 12 GREEN OVAL JUBES
- 24 BLUE MINI M&M'S

1 Spread frosting over cake tops (see tip, page 239).
2 Using picture as a guide, decorate cake tops with halved jubes to make a tortoise shell pattern. Position spearmint leaves for legs and tail, and oval jubes for head. Secure two M&M's to each head for eyes with a little frosting.

TIPS Packaged cupcakes usually come iced, however, you can ice over the top with frosting or remove the icing first. Place muffins in matching paper cases, if you like.

LEGGIT THE OCTOPUS

- ½ X 453G (14½-OUNCE) TUB VANILLA FROSTING
- YELLOW AND GREEN FOOD COLOURING SUITABLE FOR CHOCOLATE
- 3 X 460G (14½-OUNCE) PACKETS MUFFINS
- ½ CUP (75G) WHITE CHOCOLATE MELTS
- 5CM (2-INCH) ROUND CUTTER
- 12 ICE-CREAM WAFERS
- ¼ CUP GREEN SPRINKLES
- 12 WHITE MINI MARSHMALLOWS, HALVED
- 24 BROWN MINI M&M'S
- 48 RAINBOW SOUR STRAPS

1 Tint frosting yellow; spread over cake tops (see tip, page 239).
2 Melt chocolate (page 337); tint green. Using cutter, cut a round from each wafer; lay on a piece of baking paper. Spread wafers with melted chocolate, sprinkle with sprinkles. Stand until set.
3 Secure marshmallow halves and M&M's to wafers with a little melted chocolate for eyes; stand until set.
4 Cut green strips from sour straps, cut in half crossways. Repeat until you have 96 legs. Using picture as a guide, place heads upright on top of cakes; secure 8 legs around each cake.

SNAPPER THE SHARK

- 1 X 453G (14½-OUNCE) TUB VANILLA FROSTING
- BLUE AND BLACK FOOD COLOURING
- 3 X 460G (14½-OUNCE) PACKETS MUFFINS
- 5CM (2-INCH) ROUND CUTTER
- 12 ICE-CREAM WAFERS

1 Divide frosting in half. Tint half the frosting blue; spread over cake tops. Add 1 teaspoon of the reserved frosting to top of each cake; swirl the colours to look like waves.

2 Using cutter, cut a round from each wafer. Make another cut in round to form shape of a shark's fin (with a point on the bottom to push into cake).

3 Tint remaining frosting grey. Lay shark fins on a piece of baking paper; spread with grey frosting. Carefully push shark fins into centre of each cake.

TIP If using butter cream for these recipes instead of frosting, you will need to make half a quantity of butter cream (page 327); tint it the colours required by the recipe.

NIPPY THE CRAB

- ½ X 453G (14½-OUNCE) TUB VANILLA FROSTING
- ORANGE FOOD COLOURING
- 3 X 460G (14½-OUNCE) PACKETS MUFFINS
- ½ CUP (75G) WHITE CHOCOLATE MELTS
- 5CM (2-INCH) ROUND CUTTER
- 12 ICE-CREAM WAFERS
- ¼ CUP ORANGE SPRINKLES
- 24 BROWN MINI M&M'S
- 24 OVAL ORANGE JUBES
- 6 YELLOW RECTANGLE JUBES, SLICED THINLY

1 Tint frosting orange; spread over cake tops (see tip, page 239).

2 Melt chocolate (page 337). Using cutter, cut a round from each wafer; lay on a piece of baking paper. Spread wafers with melted chocolate, sprinkle with sprinkles. Stand until set.

3 Secure two M&M's to rounds for eyes with a little melted chocolate; stand until set.

4 Cut a small 'V' shape from top of each orange jube. Using picture as a guide, place chocolate rounds on top of each cake. Secure two orange jubes for claws and yellow jubes for legs.

If you want to do some baking, what do you need to get out of the fridge and the pantry? Circle the ingredients that go into a cake – cross out the ones that don't.

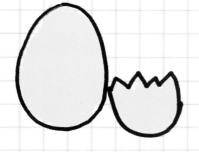

1. Eggs

2. Bread

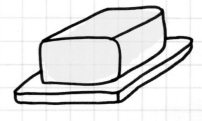

2. Butter

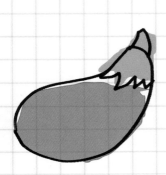

4. Eggplant

5. Broccoli

6. Flour

7. Sugar

8. Milk

9. Fish

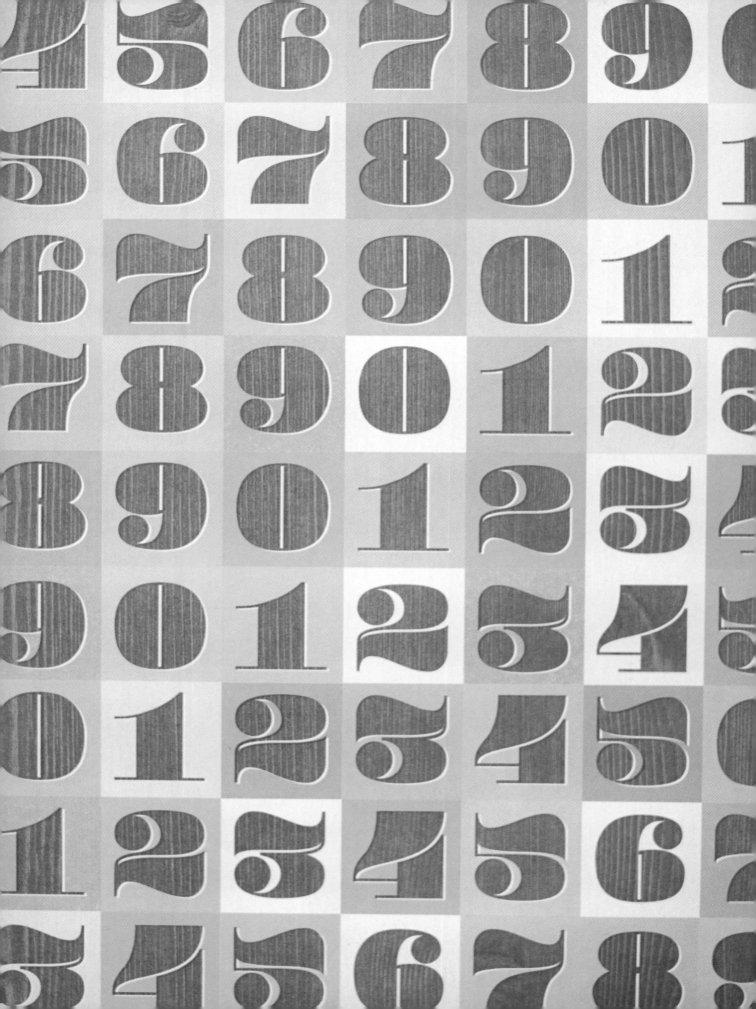

Numbers

341

NUMBER 1

1 Preheat oven to 180°C/350°F. Grease cake pan; line base with baking paper (page 332).

2 Make cakes according to directions on packets. Spread mixture into pan; bake about 45 minutes. Stand cake in pan 5 minutes before turning, top-side up, onto a wire rack to cool.

3 Using a serrated knife, level cake top (page 333). Secure cake to cake board with a little butter cream. Tint remaining butter cream blue; spread all over cake.

4 Knead ready-made icing on a surface dusted with a little sifted icing sugar until icing loses its stickiness. Roll half the icing on a surface dusted with a little icing sugar until 3mm (⅛-inch) thick. Cut an 11cm (4½-inch) square for bed sheet from icing. Shape a little of the icing trimmings into pillow.

5 Knead a little blue colouring into remaining icing; roll on a surface dusted with a little icing sugar until 3mm (⅛-inch) thick. Cut a 10cm (4-inch) square for quilt.

6 Using heart cutter, cut shapes from quilt. Position sheet on cake, top with quilt; turn down edge, as pictured. Place two heart cut-outs on pillow. Position pillow on cake.

7 Decorate cake with Smarties. Position teddy bear near cake.

TIPS Tiny heart cutters are sometimes sold as 'aspic cutters'. We've scattered sour jelly beans, milk bottles and white chocolate Melts around the cake board as decoration.

EQUIPMENT

- 23CM X 34CM (9¼-INCH X 13½-INCH) NUMBER ONE CAKE PAN
- 23CM X 51CM (9¼-INCH X 20½-INCH) RECTANGULAR CAKE BOARD (PAGE 332)
- ROLLING PIN
- 1.5CM (¾-INCH) HEART CUTTER (SEE TIPS)

CAKE

- 2 X 340G (11-OUNCE) PACKETS BUTTER CAKE MIX
- 1 QUANTITY BUTTER CREAM (PAGE 327)
- BLUE FOOD COLOURING

DECORATIONS

- 200G (6½ OUNCES) READY-MADE WHITE ICING (PAGE 327)
- PURE ICING (CONFECTIONERS') SUGAR, FOR DUSTING
- 43 SMARTIES
- SMALL TEDDY BEAR OR TOY

NUMBER 2

EQUIPMENT

- DEEP 26CM X 36CM (10½-INCH X 14½-INCH) BAKING DISH
- 12-HOLE (2-TABLESPOON/40ML) FLAT-BASED PATTY PAN
- 12 PATTY PAN PAPER CASES
- 45CM X 55CM (18-INCH X 22-INCH) RECTANGULAR CAKE BOARD (PAGE 332)

CAKE

- 3 X 340G (11-OUNCE) PACKETS BUTTER CAKE MIX
- 2 QUANTITIES BUTTER CREAM (PAGE 327)
- YELLOW, BLUE AND KELLY GREEN FOOD COLOURING

DECORATIONS

- 1.3 METRES (51-INCH) PIECE BLACK LICORICE STRAP
- 1 EACH RED, GREEN, ORANGE AND YELLOW JELLY SNAKES
- 2 WHITE CHOCOLATE MELTS
- 6 PEPPERMINT LIFE SAVERS
- 2 ORANGE GOBSTOPPERS
- 46 ORANGE SMARTIES
- 4 PURPLE KOOL FRUITS
- 1 CHOCOLATE FRECKLE
- 2 EACH GREEN AND ORANGE LOLLIPOPS
- 2 THIN SILVER CHENILLE STICKS (PIPE CLEANERS)

1 Preheat oven to 180°C/350°F. Grease baking dish; line base and sides with baking paper, extending paper 5cm (2-inch) above sides. Line patty pan with paper cases.

2 Make cakes according to directions on packets. Drop 2 tablespoons of the mixture into each paper case; bake about 20 minutes. Spread remaining mixture into baking dish; bake about 1 hour. Stand cakes in pans 5 minutes before turning, top-side up, onto wire racks to cool.

3 Using a serrated knife, level top of large cake (page 333). Secure large cake, cut-side down, to cake board with a little butter cream.

4 Tint ⅓ cup of the butter cream yellow; spread over four patty cakes. Tint ⅔ cup of the butter cream blue; spread over tops of remaining patty cakes. Tint a third of the remaining icing green;

spread over centre of large cake in a 22cm x 28cm (8¾-inch x 11¼-inch) rectangle. Tint remaining butter cream light blue; spread over sides and top of large cake as pictured. Position patty cakes around large cake.

5 Cut licorice into 2 x 22cm (¾-inch x 8¾-inch) and 2 x 28cm (11¼-inch) lengths; position on cake, using picture as a guide.

6 Cut snakes into 2cm (¾-inch) pieces, position on yellow patty cakes to form mouth. To make eyes; secure a chocolate melt, Life Saver and Gobstopper together with a little butter cream, secure on cake with butter cream.

7 Position Smarties on green icing to form a number 2. Using picture as a guide, decorate robot with Kool Fruits, freckle, lollipops and remaining Life Savers. Curl chenille sticks and attach to cake.

TIPS

To make the ballerina slippers, pictured, tie thin ribbon around milk bottles. Ballerina cake toppers are available from cake decorating suppliers.

NUMBER 3

1 Preheat oven to 180°C/350°F. Grease cake pan; line base with baking paper. Line eight holes of the patty pan with paper cases.

2 Make cakes according to directions on packets. Drop 2 tablespoons of the mixture into each paper case; bake about 20 minutes. Spread remaining mixture into cake pan; bake about 35 minutes. Stand cakes in pans 5 minutes before turning, top-side up, onto wire racks to cool.

3 Using a serrated knife, level top of number cake. Secure cake, cut-side down, to cake board with a little butter cream.

4 Tint three-quarters of the butter cream light pink; spread all over number cake. Divide remaining butter cream into four small bowls; tint medium pink, dark pink, blue and green. Using piping bags and piping tube, pipe each colour onto two patty cakes, cleaning piping tube between each colour.

5 Using picture as a guide, arrange jelly beans on patty cakes; top with ballerinas.

6 Sprinkle cake with sugar; position patty cakes on top of cake.

EQUIPMENT

- 23CM X 34CM (9¼-INCH X 13½-INCH) NUMBER THREE CAKE PAN
- 12-HOLE (2-TABLESPOON/ 40ML) FLAT-BASED PATTY PAN
- 8 PATTY PAN PAPER CASES
- 35CM X 45CM (14-INCH X 18-INCH) RECTANGULAR CAKE BOARD (PAGE 332)
- 4 SMALL DISPOSABLE PIPING BAGS
- 1 MEDIUM FLUTED PIPING TUBE

CAKE

- 3 X 340G (11-OUNCE) PACKETS BUTTER CAKE MIX
- 1½ QUANTITIES BUTTER CREAM (PAGE 327)
- ROSE PINK, SKY BLUE AND LEAF GREEN FOOD COLOURING

DECORATIONS

- 10 EACH WHITE, PINK, BLUE AND GREEN JELLY BEANS
- 8 BALLERINA CAKE TOPPERS
- 2 TABLESPOONS WHITE SUGAR CRYSTALS

NUMBER 4

EQUIPMENT

- 23CM X 34CM (9¼-INCH X 13½-INCH) NUMBER FOUR CAKE PAN
- 30CM X 40CM (12-INCH X 16-INCH) RECTANGULAR CAKE BOARD (PAGE 332)
- PAPER PIPING BAG (PAGE 336)

CAKE

- 3 X 340G (11-OUNCE) PACKETS BUTTER CAKE MIX
- 2 QUANTITIES BUTTER CREAM (PAGE 327)
- GREEN FOOD COLOURING

DECORATIONS

- 1 METRE (40-INCH) PIECE BLACK LICORICE STRAP
- 40G (1½ OUNCES) WHITE CHOCOLATE MELTS
- 4 EACH RED, ORANGE AND GREEN SMARTIES
- 4 BIRTHDAY CANDLES
- 2 X 45G (1½-OUNCE) PACKETS NEON NERDS
- 8 BLUE SMARTIES
- 6 PINEAPPLES
- 6 RACING CARS
- 2 TOY TREES

1 Preheat oven to 180°C/350°F. Grease cake pan; line base with baking paper (page 332).

2 Make cakes according to directions on packets. Spread mixture into pan; bake about 50 minutes. Stand cake in pan 5 minutes before turning, top-side up, onto a wire rack to cool.

3 Using a serrated knife, level cake top (page 333). Secure cake to the cake board with a little butter cream.

4 Tint butter cream green; spread over top and sides of cake.

5 Cut licorice to fit length and width of cake, laying two lengths side-by-side, as pictured; press onto cake.

6 Melt chocolate (page 337), spoon into piping bag; pipe road markings down centre of licorice. Attach red, orange and green Smarties to candles with melted chocolate to form traffic lights; hold in place until Smarties are secure on candles. Position traffic lights on cake.

7 Using picture as a guide, decorate cake with nerds and blue Smarties. Cut tops from pineapples to resemble bushes; arrange on cake with racing cars and toy trees.

TIPS

Racing cars and pineapples can be found in packets of party mix. If using non-edible decorations, make sure they are removed before serving.

TIPS

Peaches & cream can be found in packets of party mix. You'll have about 1 cup of the cake mixture left over; use to make extra cupcakes for the party.

NUMBER 5

1 Preheat oven to 180°C/350°F. Line 10 holes of the muffin pan with paper cases.

2 Make cake according to directions on packet. Drop 2½ level tablespoons of the mixture into each paper case; bake about 20 minutes. Stand cakes in pan 5 minutes before turning, top-side up, onto a wire rack to cool.

3 Spoon 1 tablespoon of the butter cream into a small bowl; tint yellow. Divide remaining butter cream between two small bowls; tint one grey and leave the remaining butter cream plain. Spread yellow butter cream over top of one cake; spread grey butter cream over top half of five cakes. Spread plain butter cream over bottom half of grey cakes and over top of remaining four cakes.

4 Using picture as a guide, secure cakes on cake board with a little butter cream to resemble the number 5.

5 Using yellow Smarties and chocolate Melts, decorate yellow cake to resemble cheese.

6 To decorate grey cakes as mice: position brown jelly beans for ears and pink jelly beans for noses. Cut licorice strap to make tail and whiskers; position on mice.

7 To decorate white cakes as cats: pinch peaches & cream to form a point; position, peach-side down, on cakes for ears. Position green jelly beans for eyes. Cut top from milk bottles and use to form nose. Cut remaining milk bottles to form whiskers. Position red jelly beans on cakes to form mouths

EQUIPMENT

- 12-HOLE (⅓-CUP/80ML) STANDARD MUFFIN PAN
- 10 PAPER MUFFIN CASES
- 35CM X 45CM (14-INCH X 18-INCH) RECTANGULAR CAKE BOARD (PAGE 332)

CAKE

- 1 X 340G (11-OUNCE) PACKET BUTTER CAKE MIX
- 1 QUANTITY BUTTER CREAM (PAGE 327)
- YELLOW AND BLACK FOOD COLOURING

DECORATIONS

- 3 YELLOW SMARTIES
- 3 WHITE CHOCOLATE MELTS
- 5 BROWN JELLY BEANS, HALVED LENGTHWAYS
- 3 PINK JELLY BEANS, HALVED CROSSWAYS
- 20CM (8-INCH) PIECE BLACK LICORICE STRAP
- 8 PEACHES & CREAM LOLLIES
- 4 GREEN SOUR JELLY BEANS, HALVED CROSSWAYS
- 8 CHOCOLATE MILK BOTTLES
- 2 RED JELLY BEANS, QUARTERED LENGTHWAYS

COUNT TO TEN ON YOUR FINGERS

it's easy if you try. Can you count in any other LANGUAGES? UN. DEUX. TROIS. QUATRE. CINQ...

NUMBER 6

1 Preheat oven to 180°C/350°F. Line muffin pan with paper cases.

2 Make cake according to directions on packet. Drop 2½ level tablespoons of the mixture into each paper case; bake about 20 minutes. Stand cakes in pan 5 minutes before turning, top-side up, onto a wire rack to cool.

3 Reserve 2 tablespoons of the butter cream. Divide remaining butter cream into three small bowls; tint one bowl green and one bowl blue; stir sifted cocoa into third bowl. Spread each butter cream over tops of four cakes.

4 Using picture as a guide, secure cakes on cake board with a little butter cream to resemble the number 6.

5 Decorate green cakes with nerds rope to make a trellis; intertwine with green snakes to resemble vines. Decorate with pink and green Smarties and green jelly beans.

6 Decorate brown cakes with red snakes, green jubes and strawberries & cream. Position one half only of jelly beans on one brown cake. To make mushrooms: secure chocolate Melts to white jelly beans with a little butter cream; sprinkle nerds around base of mushrooms.

7 Decorate blue cakes by placing reserved plain butter cream into paper piping bag; pipe clouds onto cakes. Quarter black and yellow jelly beans lengthways. Position red, blue and purple Smarties with quartered black jelly beans to make butterflies. Use yellow Smarties and quartered yellow jelly beans to make sun.

TIPS

Strawberries & cream can be found in packets of party mix. You'll have ¾ cup of the cake mixture left over, enough for another three cakes.

NUMBER 7

1 To make scary spiders: combine Rice Bubbles, coconut, sifted cocoa and icing sugar in a medium bowl. Stir in melted chocolate and butter. Spoon level tablespoons of the mixture into mini muffin pan holes. Refrigerate 1 hour or until spiders have set.

2 Preheat oven to 180°C/350°F. Grease cake pan; line base with baking paper (page 332).

3 Make cakes according to directions on packets. Spread mixture into cake pan; bake about 45 minutes. Stand cake in pan 5 minutes before turning, top-side up, onto a wire rack to cool.

4 Using a serrated knife, level cake top (page 333). Secure cake to cake board with a little butter cream. Tint butter cream purple; spread all over cake.

5 To decorate scary spiders, place melted chocolate into piping bag. Using picture as a guide, pipe spider webs onto cake and cake board. Pipe spider legs onto a sheet of baking paper; leave for 15 minutes or until set.

6 Position eight spider bodies on and around cake; secure legs to bodies with a little melted chocolate.

7 Using leftover butter cream, attach Smarties to spiders for eyes; pipe pupils on Smarties with writing gel.

TIPS Dark chocolate Melts and butter can be melted together over hot water or in the microwave on HIGH (100%) about 1 minute. This recipe makes 17 scary spider bodies, however, the decorations listed are for the eight spiders pictured. Serve the extras as an accompaniment or, if you have extra chocolate Melts and Smarties, make more spiders to decorate the cake board or to give to each guest. The butterflies used in the picture are store-bought trinkets; add whatever spider food you like to the spider webs. If using non-edible decorations, make sure they are removed before serving.

EQUIPMENT

- 2 X 12-HOLE (1-TABLESPOON/ 20ML) MINI MUFFIN PANS
- 20CM X 34CM (8-INCH X 13½-INCH) NUMBER SEVEN CAKE PAN
- 30CM X 50CM (12-INCH X 20-INCH) RECTANGULAR CAKE BOARD (PAGE 332)
- PAPER PIPING BAG (PAGE 336)

CAKE

- 2 X 340G (11-OUNCE) PACKETS BUTTER CAKE MIX
- 1½ QUANTITIES BUTTER CREAM (PAGE 327)
- PURPLE FOOD COLOURING

SCARY SPIDERS

- 1 CUP (35G) RICE BUBBLES
- 1 CUP (70G) SHREDDED COCONUT
- 1 TABLESPOON COCOA POWDER
- 1 TABLESPOON ICING (CONFECTIONERS') SUGAR
- 100G (3 OUNCES) DARK CHOCOLATE MELTS, MELTED (PAGE 337)
- 30G BUTTER, MELTED

DECORATIONS

- 150G (4½ OUNCES) DARK CHOCOLATE MELTS, MELTED (PAGE 337)
- 16 SMARTIES, TWO OF EACH COLOUR
- BLACK GLITTER WRITING GEL

NUMBER 8

EQUIPMENT

- 23CM X 34CM (9¼-INCH X 13½-INCH) NUMBER EIGHT CAKE PAN
- 30CM X 48CM (12-INCH X 19¼-INCH) RECTANGULAR CAKE BOARD (PAGE 332)

CAKE

- 3 X 340G (11-OUNCE) PACKETS BUTTER CAKE MIX
- 2 QUANTITIES BUTTER CREAM (PAGE 327)
- ORANGE AND AQUA FOOD COLOURING

DECORATIONS

- 8 KILLER PYTHONS
- 1 ORANGE JELLY SNAKE
- 2 RED SMARTIES
- 2 WHITE CHOCOLATE MELTS
- 13 ROUND JUBES
- 10 BLUE SMARTIES

1 Preheat oven to 180°C/350°F. Grease cake pan; line base with baking paper (page 332).

2 Make cakes according to directions on packets. Spread mixture into cake pan; bake about 1 hour. Stand cake in pan 5 minutes before turning, top-side up, onto a wire rack to cool.

3 Using a serrated knife, level cake top (page 333). Secure cake, cut-side down, to cake board with a little butter cream.

4 Reserve 1 teaspoon of the butter cream. Tint half the remaining butter cream orange; spread over top and side of top cake half. Tint remaining butter cream aqua; spread over top and side of bottom cake half.

5 Cut heads from Killer Pythons and snake. Using picture as a guide, position pythons around centre of cake for octopus tentacles; press gently into butter cream. Position snake across top of pythons.

6 Using a little reserved butter cream, attach red Smarties to chocolate Melts to make eyes; position on cake.

7 Decorate head of octopus with jubes and blue Smarties.

TIP You will need 2 x 180g (5½-ounce) packets of Killer Pythons.

TIP
Milk bottles, Killer Pythons, snakes, teeth and racing cars can be found in packets of party mix.

NUMBER 9

1 Preheat oven to 180°C/350°F. Grease cake pan; line base with baking paper (page 332).

2 Make cakes according to directions on packets. Spread mixture into pan; bake about 50 minutes. Stand cake in pan 5 minutes before turning, top-side up, onto a wire rack to cool.

3 Using a serrated knife, level cake top (page 333). Secure cake to the cake board with a little butter cream.

4 Tint butter cream green; spread over top and sides of cake.

5 Cut snakes on a diagonal at different lengths. Cut green sections from Killer Python (you will need three pieces). Cut 'V' shapes from teeth to make pointy teeth.

6 Position lollies on cake to form a fire-breathing dragon, as pictured.

EQUIPMENT

- 22CM X 34CM (8¾-INCH X 13½-INCH) NUMBER NINE CAKE PAN
- 30CM X 40CM (12-INCH X 16-INCH) RECTANGULAR CAKE BOARD (PAGE 332)

CAKE

- 3 X 340G (11-OUNCE) PACKETS BUTTER CAKE MIX
- 2 QUANTITIES BUTTER CREAM (PAGE 327)
- GREEN FOOD COLOURING

DECORATIONS

- 12 (TOTAL) ORANGE, RED AND YELLOW JELLY SNAKES
- 1 KILLER PYTHON
- 2 JELLY TEETH
- 11 RACING CARS
- 1 JAFFA
- 2 LIME MILK BOTTLES

NUMBER

10

EQUIPMENT

- 15CM X 34CM (6-INCH X 13½-INCH) NUMBER ONE CAKE PAN
- 23CM X 34CM (9¼-INCH X 13½-INCH) NUMBER ZERO CAKE PAN
- 90CM SQUARE (35-INCH) CAKE BOARD (PAGE 332)

CAKE

- 5 X 340G (11-OUNCE) PACKETS BUTTER CAKE MIX
- 3 QUANTITIES BUTTER CREAM (PAGE 327)
- YELLOW FOOD COLOURING

DECORATIONS

- 12 RED JELLY SNAKES
- 2 RED JELLY BEANS
- 2 ORANGE JELLY BEANS
- 6 GREEN JELLY BEANS
- 2 YELLOW JELLY BEANS
- 10 PINK JELLY BEANS
- 5 PURPLE JELLY BEANS
- 4 WHITE JELLY BEANS
- 4 GREEN SOUR JELLY BEANS
- 10 GREEN JUBES
- 5 ORANGE JUBES
- 3 WHITE JUBES
- 4 JELLY RASPBERRIES
- 2 TABLESPOONS GRAPE NERDS

1 Preheat oven to 180°C/350°F. Grease cake pans; line bases with baking paper (page 332).

2 Make cakes according to directions on packets. Spread mixture evenly into pans. Bake number 1 cake about 45 minutes; bake number 0 cake for about 50 minutes. Stand cakes in pans for 10 minutes before turning, top-side up, onto wire racks to cool.

3 Using a serrated knife, level cake tops so cakes are same height. Secure cakes to cake board with a little butter cream. Tint butter cream yellow; spread all over top and sides of cakes.

4 Using kitchen scissors, cut heads from snakes; tie tails into knots. Cut red and orange jelly beans into quarters. Cut remaining jelly beans and jubes in half lengthways. Using picture as a guide, arrange snakes, jelly beans, jubes, raspberries and nerds (see tip) on cakes.

TIP Use a pair of clean tweezers to position nerds and other small lollies, if you like.

MIRROR WRITING

Hold this page up to the mirror. Can you read the secret message?

ON YOUR
BIRTHDAY YOU
GET TO EAT CAKE
FOR BREAKFAST,
LUNCH AND
DINNER

SECRET CODE

Match the numbers to the letters to crack the code. Hint: You get to eat a lot of these on your birthday.

12 15 12 12 9 5 19   1 14 4

3 8 15 3 15 12 1 20 5

1 14 4

19 16 18 9 14 11 12 5 19

1 = A	6 = F	11 = K	16 = P	20 = T	24 = X
2 = B	7 = G	12 = L	17 = Q	21 = U	25 = Y
3 = C	8 = H	13 = M	18 = R	22 = V	26 = Z
4 = D	9 = I	14 = N	19 = S	23 = W	
5 = E	10 = J	15 = O			

ANSWER: LOLLIES AND CHOCOLATE AND SPRINKLES

Fantasy

TIPS

Bananas and racing cars can be found in packets of party mix. You will need about 6 x 170g (5½-ounce) packets of milk bottles.

DAN THE DRAGON

1 Preheat oven to 180°C/350°F. Grease cake pan, dust lightly with flour; shake off excess (page 332).

2 Make cakes according to directions on packets. Spread mixture into pan; bake about 45 minutes. Stand cake in pan 5 minutes before turning, top-side up, onto wire rack to cool.

3 Trim bottom of cake, so cake lies flat. Secure cake on cake board with a little butter cream.

4 Tint butter cream yellow; spread all over cake.

5 Cut teeth to make pointy. Position on cake, using picture as a guide. Discard head from snake; position snake body on cake to form tongue. Position jelly bean as nose, strawberries & cream as eye and banana as eyebrow.

6 Cut milk bottles lengthways into three strips; position on cake for scales.

7 Cut racing cars into triangles, position down dinosaur's back for spikes. Cut jelly babies into triangles to represent claws.

EQUIPMENT

- 27CM X 31CM (10¾-INCH X 12½-INCH) DINOSAUR CAKE PAN
- 31CM X 45CM (12½ INCH X 18-INCH) RECTANGULAR CAKE BOARD (PAGE 332)

CAKE

- 2 X 340G (11-OUNCE) PACKETS BUTTER CAKE MIX
- 1½ QUANTITIES BUTTER CREAM (PAGE 327)
- BUTTERCUP YELLOW COLOURING

DECORATIONS

- 4 JELLY TEETH
- 1 RED JELLY SNAKE
- 1 CHOCOLATE MILKSHAKE JELLY BEAN
- 1 STRAWBERRIES & CREAM LOLLY
- 1 YELLOW BANANA LOLLY
- 40 BANANA MILK BOTTLES
- 16 GREEN RACING CARS
- 6 CHOCOLATE JELLY BABIES

CUPID'S CUPCAKES

EQUIPMENT

- THREE 12-HOLE (⅓-CUP/80ML) STANDARD MUFFIN PANS
- 25 PAPER MUFFIN CASES
- 5 DISPOSABLE PIPING BAGS
- MEDIUM PLAIN PIPING TUBE (SEE TIPS)
- 48CM X 55CM (19¼-INCH X 22-INCH) RECTANGULAR CAKE BOARD (PAGE 332)

CAKE

- 2 X 340G (11-OUNCE) PACKETS BUTTER CAKE MIX
- 2 QUANTITIES BUTTER CREAM (PAGE 327)
- PINK FOOD COLOURING

DECORATIONS

- 8 RED JUBES
- 4 RED JELLY SNAKES
- 1 BANANA MILK BOTTLE
- 3 STRAWBERRY MILK BOTTLES
- 6 PEPPERMINT LIFE SAVERS, HALVED
- 6 MUSK LIFE SAVERS, HALVED
- 4 JELLY RASPBERRIES
- 3 WHITE JUBES, HALVED
- 3 CHOCOLATE FRECKLES
- 6 TANGY TOFFEE APPLE, BUTTER POPCORN AND FAIRY FLOSS JELLY BEANS
- 6 GRAPEFRUIT SOUR JELLY BEANS
- 4 PINK SMARTIES
- 4 GREEN JUBES, HALVED
- PINK SANDING SUGAR

1 Preheat oven to 180°C/350°F. Line 25 holes of the muffin pans with paper cases.

2 Make cakes according to directions on packets. Divide mixture evenly among paper cases; bake about 20 minutes. Stand cakes in pans 5 minutes before turning, top-side up, onto wire racks to cool.

3 Divide butter cream into 5 bowls. Keep one bowl plain; tint remaining butter cream in four different shades of pink.

4 Spoon plain butter cream into one of the piping bags fitted with piping tube; pipe onto five cakes. Repeat with remaining colours.

5 Cut 5 red jubes in half crossways. Remove heads from snakes; tie tails into a knot. Cut and keep bottle top tip from top of milk bottles (discard bottle bases). Using picture as a guide, decorate cakes with Life Savers and lollies. Sprinkle with sanding sugar.

6 Arrange cupcakes, side by side, on cake board, in the shape of a heart.

TIPS Wash and dry the piping tube between each coloured butter cream. Coloured butter cream can become lighter or darker on standing. If you have time, colour a small amount of the butter cream, then cover it with plastic wrap and allow it to stand for a few hours to determine if the colour fades or darkens. Plain butter cream is a cream colour, so when red or pink colours are added, the butter cream may appear to be apricot or salmon in colour.

HAPPY HOBBITS'
HOLIDAY HOUSE

1 Using a little frosting, stack cakes together. Using a serrated knife, trim into a dome shape. Position two of the muffins on either side of cake, with flat muffin bases against cake. Cut remaining muffin in half, crossways. Position cut muffin on either side of one of the whole muffins to form a mound. Spread frosting over top and sides of cake and muffins.

2 Melt the chocolate (page 337). Divide chocolate into two small bowls. Tint one portion blue and other portion green. Spread one of the Wagon Wheels with blue chocolate and remaining Wagon Wheel with green chocolate. Using picture as a guide; top green Wagon Wheel with M&M and the blue Wagon Wheel with licorice strap. Allow to set.

3 Using picture as a guide, position Wagon Wheels on cake for door and window. Secure chocolate bullets and sultanas on front of cake. Position spearmint leaves and bootlaces on top of cake.

4 Position Ovalteenies for pathway. Tint the coconut green (page 336). Sprinkle coconut on back of cake and around base of cake.

EQUIPMENT

- 30CM (12-INCH) ROUND CAKE BOARD (PAGE 332)

CAKE

- 1 X 453G (14½-OUNCE) TUB MILK CHOCOLATE FROSTING
- 2 X 450G (14½-OUNCE) PACKETS CHOCOLATE DOUBLE SPONGE ROUNDS
- 3 X CHOCOLATE CHIP MUFFINS

DECORATIONS

- 50G (1½ OUNCES) WHITE CHOCOLATE MELTS
- BLUE AND GREEN FOOD COLOURING SUITABLE FOR CHOCOLATE
- 2 X 190G (6-OUNCE) PACKETS MINI CHOCOLATE WAGON WHEELS
- 1 ORANGE MINI M&M
- 6CM (2½-INCH) PIECE BLACK LICORICE STRAP, CUT INTO THIN STRIPS
- 36 MILK CHOCOLATE LICORICE BULLETS
- 30 CHOCOLATE-COVERED SULTANAS
- 200G (6½-OUNCE) PACKET SPEARMINT LEAVES, HALVED HORIZONTALLY
- 4 GREEN BOOTLACES
- 3 X 15G (½-OUNCE) PACKETS OVALTEENIES
- 1 CUP (80G) DESICCATED COCONUT

DISCO
DIVA

EQUIPMENT

- **DEEP 26CM X 36CM (10½-INCH X 14½-INCH) BAKING DISH**
- **30CM X 46CM (12-INCH X 18½-INCH) RECTANGULAR CAKE BOARD (PAGE 332)**

CAKE

- **3 X 340G (11-OUNCE) PACKETS BUTTER CAKE MIX**
- **2½ QUANTITIES BUTTER CREAM (PAGE 327)**
- **PINK FOOD COLOURING**

DECORATIONS

- **3 RED JELLY SNAKES**
- **1 EACH ORANGE, YELLOW AND GREEN JELLY SNAKES**
- **2CM (¾-INCH) SILVER DISCO BALL**
- **SILVER EDIBLE GLITTER**
- **52 JUBES**
- **1.3 METRES (51-INCH) SILVER SEQUINED RIBBON**

1 Preheat oven to 180°C/350°F. Grease baking dish; line base and sides with baking paper, extending paper 5cm (2-inch) above sides.

2 Make cakes according to directions on packets. Spread into dish; bake about 1 hour. Stand cake 20 minutes before turning, top-side up, onto a wire rack to cool.

3 Using a serrated knife, level cake top (page 333). Secure cake, cut-side down, on cake board with a little butter cream.

4 Tint butter cream pink; spread all over cake.

5 Remove heads from snakes. Using picture as a guide, cut and arrange snake tails to make the word 'Disco', dipping some cut ends into a little water and then into edible glitter. Position disco ball above the 'i'. Sprinkle edible glitter over top of cake.

6 Position jubes around top of cake. Wrap ribbon around base of cake.

TIPS
Edible glitter is available from specialist cake decorating shops. You will need 2 x 190g (6-ounce) packets of jubes.

TIPS

House can be assembled
3 days ahead. Give the kids
a surprise by filling the house
with lollies before putting
on the roof. The black cat
is available in packets
of party mix.

GINGERBREAD HOUSE

1 To make gingerbread; process flour, spices and butter until mixture is crumbly (you may need to do this in two batches). Add sugar, treacle and enough egg for mixture to just combine. Turn dough onto a floured surface; knead until smooth. Cover; refrigerate 1 hour.

2 To make cardboard patterns: cut two 12cm x 19cm (4¾-inch x 7¾-inch) rectangles for roof; two 10.5cm x 16cm (4-inch x 6½-inch) rectangles for side walls and two 16cm x 18cm (6½-inch x 7¼-inch) rectangles for front and back walls. Trim front and back walls to form two 11cm (4½-inch) high gables (pointy top).

3 Preheat oven to 180°C/350°F. Roll dough between sheets of baking paper until 5mm (¼-inch) thick. Peel away top paper; use cardboard patterns to cut shapes from dough. Pull away excess dough; slide baking paper with shapes onto oven trays. Re-roll dough scraps until 5mm (¼-inch) thick; cut out a freehand tree and use cutter to cut a flower shape. Bake, uncovered, for 12 minutes or until shapes are just firm (they will become crisp after they cool).

4 While shapes are still warm and soft, use tip of a sharp knife to cut out windows from side walls, and a door from front wall; reserve cut-out door. Trim shapes to straighten sides; transfer all shapes to wire racks to cool.

5 Secure two crossed skewers to back of each roof piece with a little royal icing. Allow to dry.

6 To assemble house: secure roof and walls together with royal icing. Stand house on cake board for several hours, or overnight if possible, supporting sides with four cans, to keep upright, so it is thoroughly dry before decorating. Secure door and flower to house with royal icing.

7 Using picture as a guide, decorate house with lollies, securing with royal icing. Secure tree to cake board; decorate with green jubes for leaves. Form a path with yellow Smarties.

EQUIPMENT

- THIN CARDBOARD
- 3 OVEN TRAYS
- 5.5CM (2¼-INCH) FLOWER COOKIE CUTTER
- 4 BAMBOO SKEWERS
- 35CM (14-INCH) SQUARE CAKE BOARD (PAGE 332)

GINGERBREAD

- 4½ CUPS (675G) SELF-RAISING FLOUR
- 3 TEASPOONS GROUND GINGER
- 2 TEASPOONS GROUND CINNAMON
- 1½ TEASPOONS GROUND CLOVES
- 1 TEASPOON GROUND NUTMEG
- 185G (6 OUNCES) COLD BUTTER, CHOPPED
- 1 CUP (220G) FIRMLY PACKED DARK BROWN SUGAR
- ½ CUP (180G) TREACLE
- 2 EGGS, BEATEN LIGHTLY
- 1 QUANTITY ROYAL ICING (PAGE 327)

DECORATIONS

- 84 CHOCOLATE FRECKLES
- 1 RED JELLY SNAKE, FOR WINDOW SILLS
- 3 YELLOW JELLY SNAKES, TRIMMED
- 8 JUBES
- 8 SMARTIES
- 2 WHITE MILK BOTTLES
- 1 JELLY BLACK CAT
- 6 GREEN JUBES, HALVED
- YELLOW SMARTIES

THE LITTLEST PRINCESS

EQUIPMENT

- 12 PINK AND WHITE STANDARD PAPER CASES
- LARGE PIPING BAG FITTED WITH A 1.5CM (¾-INCH) FLUTED TUBE

CAKE

- 12 DOUBLE CHOCOLATE-CHIP MUFFINS
- 1 X 453G (14½-OUNCE) TUB VANILLA FROSTING
- PURPLE AND PINK FOOD COLOURING

DECORATIONS

- 120CM (4-FEET) ROLL PURPLE BUBBLE GUM TAPE
- 1 TABLESPOON PINK SPRINKLES
- 2 TABLESPOONS PINK SANDING SUGAR

1 Place muffins in paper cases.

2 To make crowns: cut 12 x 10cm (4-inch) lengths of bubble gum tape; wipe excess powder from strips. Using picture as a guide, use a small sharp knife to cut 5mm (¼-inch) high triangles, side-by-side, from top of each bubble gum strip to make tips of crown. Dip one end of each strip in a little water, secure ends together, pinching to seal. Fan tips of crown outwards.

3 Place sprinkles in a small bowl. Place a little water in another small bowl. Dip tips of crowns quickly in water, shake off excess water; dip in sprinkles.

4 Tint frosting purple using purple and a little pink colouring. Spoon frosting into piping bag; pipe frosting onto each muffin. Sprinkle with sanding sugar; top with crowns.

TIP
We used plain, mini and domed-shaped white marshmallows to decorate the cake board with snow.

SO, YOU WANT TO BUILD A SNOWMAN

1 Cut one of the cakes into a 12cm (4¾-inch) round using plate as a guide. Secure cakes, as pictured, on cake board with a little frosting. Place cakes in freezer until firm.

2 Reserve 2 tablespoons of the frosting for decorating. Spread remaining frosting over top and sides of cakes. Sprinkle cake with coconut.

3 Melt white chocolate in a small bowl over a saucepan of simmering water (page 337); stir in oil, then tint chocolate orange. Roll waffle cone in chocolate; place on a piece of baking paper to set.

4 Trim sour straps; attach to cake for scarf. Reserve leftover sour strap.

5 Using picture as a guide; position chocolate Melts on smaller cake for eyes, top with marshmallows then M&Ms, securing with a little frosting as needed. Position fruit rings for buttons and waffle cone for nose. Position mini M&M's for mouth. Push pretzels in sides of cake for arms.

6 To make hat: cut muffin bar in half lengthways through centre; cut one long piece in half crossways. Secure smaller pieces on top of each other, then secure to centre of larger piece. Position on top of snowman with a little frosting. Spread frosting over top and sides of hat. Cut licorice strap into strips to neatly fit on top and around sides of muffin. Cut a piece of reserved sour strap and position around hat for hat band.

TIP Cut licorice strap from centre of strap roll where it has been wound tightly, so you get a rounded shape for the hat.

EQUIPMENT
- 15CM PLATE
- 30CM X 40XM (12-INCH X 16-INCH) RECTANGULAR CAKE BOARD (PAGE 332)

CAKE
- 1 X 460G (14½-OUNCE) PACKET DOUBLE UNFILLED SPONGE CAKE ROUNDS
- 1½ X 453G (14½-OUNCE) TUBS VANILLA FROSTING
- 1 X 42G (1½-OUNCE) MUFFIN BAR

DECORATIONS
- ⅔ CUP (50G) SHREDDED COCONUT
- 50G (1½ OUNCES) WHITE CHOCOLATE, CHOPPED
- A FEW DROPS VEGETABLE OIL
- ORANGE FOOD COLOURING
- 1 MINI WAFFLE ICE-CREAM CONE
- 3 RED SOUR STRAPS
- 2 DARK CHOCOLATE MELTS
- 2 WHITE MARSHMALLOWS
- 2 BROWN M&M'S
- 3 GREEN SOUR FRUIT RINGS
- 6 BROWN MINI M&M'S
- 4 PRETZEL RODS
- 28CM (11¼ INCHES) BLACK LICORICE STRAP

DOUGHNUT STACK

1 Place doughnuts on wire rack over oven tray. Divide frosting among two microwave-safe bowls; tint one pink and one green.

2 Microwave pink frosting on high (100%) for 15 seconds or until melted. Spoon frosting over half the doughnuts. Repeat with green frosting and remaining doughnuts. Decorate pink doughnuts with white sprinkles and green doughnuts with pink sprinkles.

3 Stack doughnuts on cake board.

TIP For an even faster cake, buy a variety of iced doughnuts in different colours, and secure them together with a little vanilla frosting.

EQUIPMENT

- WIRE RACK
- OVEN TRAY
- 25CM (10-INCH) ROUND CAKE BOARD (PAGE 332)

CAKE

- 12 CINNAMON DOUGHNUTS
- 1 X 453G (14½-OUNCE) TUB VANILLA FROSTING
- PINK AND GREEN FOOD COLOURING

DECORATIONS

- ⅓ CUP (65G) WHITE SPRINKLES
- ⅓ CUP (65G) PINK SPRINKLES

UMBELIEVABLE
UMBRELLA

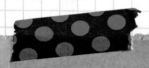

EQUIPMENT

- DEEP 30CM (12-INCH) ROUND CAKE PAN
- 5.5CM (2¼-INCH) AND 3CM (1¼-INCH) ROUND CUTTERS
- 40CM (16-INCH) SQUARE CAKE BOARD (PAGE 332)

CAKE

- 4 X 340G (11-OUNCE) PACKETS BUTTER CAKE MIX
- 2 QUANTITIES BUTTER CREAM (PAGE 327)
- YELLOW FOOD COLOURING

DECORATIONS

- HUNDREDS & THOUSANDS
- 8 JAFFAS
- 35 WHITE MILK BOTTLES, HALVED
- 36 LIME MILK BOTTLES, HALVED
- 19 BANANA MILK BOTTLES, HALVED

1 Preheat oven to 180°C/350°F. Grease cake pan; line base with baking paper (page 332).

2 Make cakes according to directions on packets. Spread mixture into pan; bake about 1½ hours. Stand cake in pan 5 minutes before turning, top-side up, onto a wire rack to cool.

3 Using a serrated knife, level top of the cake (page 333); turn cake cut-side down. Cut a third off cake; reserve.

4 Using picture as a guide, cut 5 scallop shapes into cut edge of large piece of cake using 5.5cm cutter. Secure cake on cake board with a little butter cream. Tint butter cream yellow; spread all over cake.

5 Cut seven rounds from reserved cake using 3cm cutter to make umbrella's handle (see tips). Working with one round at a time, spread butter cream over side of each round; roll side in hundreds & thousands. Secure to cake board with a little butter cream. Spread top of rounds with yellow butter cream; top with a Jaffa.

6 Decorate top of umbrella with milk bottles; top with remaining Jaffa.

TIPS The cutters we used were about 5cm (2-inch) deep, which made it easier to cut right through the cake. You could use a sharp pointed knife to cut out the cake rounds, cutting around the markings of a shorter cutter. Freeze the cake rounds for about an hour to help prevent them from crumbling while icing.

PRINCESS PHOEBE'S
CASTLE

1 Preheat oven to 180°C/350°F. Grease cake pans; line bases with baking paper (page 332). Line five holes of the muffin pan with paper cases.

2 Make cakes according to directions on packets. Three-quarters fill paper cases with mixture; bake about 20 minutes. Pour enough of the remaining mixture into square and round pans so they are three-quarters full; bake about 1 hour. Stand cakes in pans 5 minutes before turning, top-side up, onto wire racks to cool.

3 Using a serrated knife, level tops of square cakes so they are same height (page 333). Using a little butter cream, sandwich square cakes together. Using a serrated knife, level top of round cake; turn cake cut-side down.

4 Secure square cake to cake board with a little butter cream (allowing space for drawbridge). Using one of the biscuits as a guide, cut rounds out of each corner of square cake with a small serrated knife. Secure round cake to top of square cake with a little butter cream.

5 Tint three-quarters of the butter cream green. Spread all over cakes. Stack six biscuits, joining each with a little butter cream, in each cut-out corner. Tint remaining butter cream yellow, spoon into piping bag; pipe onto each cupcake. Position one cupcake on top of each biscuit stack, and one on top of castle to make towers.

6 Gently push lollipops into each tower; position flags. Using picture as a guide, position milk bottles, jelly babies, Kool Fruits, freckles and 17 jubes on cake.

7 Using kitchen scissors, trim wafers into shapes for door and drawbridge; position on cake. To make chains for drawbridge; cut skewers to about 12cm (4¾-inch). Slide Life Savers onto skewers, finishing with remaining two jubes; position on cake, securing with a little butter cream.

TIPS Flavoured milk bottles can be found in packets of milk bottles; use whichever colours you like. Be sure to remove the skewers from the cake before serving.

EQUIPMENT

- TWO DEEP 23CM (9¼-INCH) SQUARE CAKE PANS
- DEEP 15CM (6-INCH) ROUND CAKE PAN
- 12-HOLE (⅓-CUP/80ML) STANDARD MUFFIN PAN
- 5 PAPER MUFFIN CASES
- 36CM (14½-INCH) SQUARE CAKE BOARD (PAGE 332)
- PIPING BAG FITTED WITH A LARGE STAR PIPING TUBE
- 2 BAMBOO SKEWERS

CAKE

- 5 X 340G (11-OUNCE) PACKETS BUTTER CAKE MIX
- 4 QUANTITIES BUTTER CREAM (PAGE 327)
- KELLY GREEN AND YELLOW FOOD COLOURING

DECORATIONS

- 1½ X 250G (8-OUNCE) PACKETS ORANGE CREAM BISCUITS
- 4 RED LOLLIPOPS
- 1 GREEN LOLLIPOP
- 4 FLAG CAKE TOPPERS
- 35 MILK BOTTLES
- 20 CHOCOLATE JELLY BABIES, HALVED
- 35 KOOL FRUITS
- 13 CHOCOLATE FRECKLES
- 19 JUBES
- 4 ICE-CREAM WAFERS
- 2 X 34G (1-OUNCE) PACKETS FIVE FLAVOURS LIFE SAVERS

INTO THE FAIRY FOREST

EQUIPMENT

- 20CM X 25CM (8-INCH X 10-INCH) RECTANGULAR CAKE BOARD (PAGE 332)

CAKE

- 1 X 500G (1-POUND) PACKET HONEY SPONGE ROLL
- 1 X 238G (7½-OUNCE) CAN PETAL PINK SOFT FROSTING

DECORATIONS

- 2 X 16G (½-OUNCE) PACKET PANSY ICING FLOWERS
- ½ X 19G (¾-OUNCE) PACKET ROSE ICING FLOWERS

1 Secure cake to cake board with a little frosting. Place fluted nozzle on frosting can and pipe rosettes all over top and sides of cake.

2 Decorate cake with icing flowers.

TIP You can use a tub of strawberry frosting, if you prefer; place frosting in a piping bag fitted with a small fluted piping tube to pipe the rosettes.

PARTY PIÑATA

1 Preheat oven to 180°C/350°F. Grease cake pan; line base with baking paper (page 332).

2 Make cake according to directions on packet. Spread into pan until three-quarters full; bake about 45 minutes. Stand cake in pan 5 minutes before turning, top-side up, onto a wire rack to cool.

3 Secure cake on cake board with a little butter cream. Using ruler and toothpicks, mark an 11cm (4½-inch) circle in centre of cake. Using markings as a guide, cut a deep hollow into cake with a small serrated knife.

4 Spread butter cream all over cake; allow to set, then fill hollow with lollies.

5 To make piñata shell; grease pudding steamer with oil; place bowl in freezer for 10 minutes. Meanwhile, melt chocolate (page 337); pour into steamer, swirl chocolate to coat inside of steamer evenly. Continue swirling until chocolate begins to set and stops flowing around steamer (keep chocolate a uniform thickness, particularly at top edge). Stand until chocolate is almost set. Freeze until chocolate sets completely.

6 Carefully place steamer with set piñata shell over cake; using a hot cloth, briefly rub outside of steamer – piñata shell should slip from bowl to enclose cake.

7 Melt the extra chocolate (page 337); secure Smarties and Gobstoppers to piñata shell with a little melted chocolate.

8 Allow birthday child to break piñata shell open with toy hammer.

TIP We used Fantales, party mix lollies, Kool Fruits, chocolate freckles, jelly beans, Smarties and Gobstoppers to fill and decorate this cake.

EQUIPMENT

- DEEP 15CM (6-INCH) ROUND CAKE PAN
- 2.25-LITRE (9-CUP) PUDDING STEAMER
- 30CM (12-INCH) ROUND CAKE BOARD (PAGE 332)
- RULER
- WOODEN TOOTHPICKS

CAKE

- 1 X 340G (11-OUNCE) PACKET BUTTER CAKE MIX
- 1 QUANTITY CHOCOLATE BUTTER CREAM (PAGE 327)

PIÑATA SHELL

- ½ TEASPOON VEGETABLE OIL
- 450G (14½ OUNCES) MILK CHOCOLATE MELTS

DECORATIONS

- ASSORTED LOLLIES (SEE TIP)
- 50G (1½ OUNCES) MILK CHOCOLATE MELTS, EXTRA
- 1½ X 190G (6-OUNCE) PACKETS SMARTIES
- 1 X 50G (1½-OUNCE) PACKET GOBSTOPPERS
- TOY HAMMER

TINY FAERIES FROLICKING

EQUIPMENT
- 3 DISPOSABLE PLASTIC PIPING BAGS

CAKE
- 12 DOUBLE CHOCOLATE-CHIP MUFFINS OR CUPCAKES
- 1 X 453G (14½-OUNCE) TUB VANILLA FROSTING

DECORATIONS
- 150G (4½ OUNCES) WHITE CHOCOLATE
- GREEN, PINK AND PURPLE FOOD COLOURING SUITABLE FOR CHOCOLATE
- ¼ CUP PINK SUGAR PEARLS
- GREEN, PINK AND PURPLE SANDING SUGAR
- 24 SMALL GREEN APPLE FRUIT RINGS
- 24 PINK SWEETHEART LOLLIES
- 12 SMALL DOLLS

1 Remove paper cases from muffins; cut muffins in half crossways. Spread frosting over cut side of muffins. Attach two halves together at flat base of muffins, joining in centre.

2 Melt the chocolate (page 337). Divide chocolate into three small bowls; tint green, pink and purple. Spoon melted chocolate into piping bags; snip a small hole at end of bags. Using picture as a guide, pipe patterns onto wings. Decorate with sugar pearls, sanding sugar, fruit rings and sweetheart lollies.

3 Place dolls in centre of wings.

TIPS Freeze the cut muffins for 1 hour before icing, this will prevent crumbs from getting into the frosting. We used Polly Pocket dolls available from toy stores and supermarkets; remove before serving.

LOLLY DOLLY

1 Preheat oven to 180°C/350°F. Grease pudding steamer well.

2 Make cakes according to directions on packets. Spread mixture into steamer; bake about 1 hour. Stand cake in steamer 5 minutes before turning onto a wire rack to cool.

3 Level base of cake to sit flat. Secure cake to cake board with a little butter cream.

4 Tint butter cream pink; spread all over cake. Gently push doll down into cake to waist level; spread butter cream over doll to form a bodice.

5 Trim one snake; outline bodice. Using picture as a guide, and starting from bottom, decorate skirt and bodice with milk bottles and raspberries. Trim remaining snakes to outline front of skirt between raspberries and milk bottles.

TIPS Flavoured milk bottles can be found in packets of milk bottles; you will need about 3 x 170g (5½-ounce) packets. If using non-edible decorations, make sure they are removed before serving.

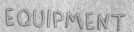

EQUIPMENT

- 2-LITRE (8-CUP) PUDDING STEAMER
- 30CM (12-INCH) ROUND CAKE BOARD (PAGE 332)

CAKE

- 2 X 340G (11-OUNCE) PACKETS BUTTER CAKE MIX
- 1 QUANTITY BUTTER CREAM (PAGE 327)
- PINK FOOD COLOURING

DECORATIONS

- 1 DOLL, LEGS REMOVED
- 3 RED JELLY SNAKES
- 17 WHITE MILK BOTTLES
- 13 STRAWBERRY MILK BOTTLES
- 2 X 190G (6-OUNCE) PACKETS JELLY RASPBERRIES, HALVED

PRINCESS OF HEARTS

EQUIPMENT

- 25CM X 35CM (10-INCH X 14-INCH) RECTANGULAR CAKE BOARD (PAGE 332)
- 5CM (2-INCH) AND 3CM (1¼-INCH) HEART CUTTERS

CAKE

- 1 X 450G (14½-OUNCE) PACKAGED DOUBLE UNFILLED SPONGE SLABS
- 1 X 453G (14½-OUNCE) TUB STRAWBERRY FROSTING

DECORATIONS

- 1 TABLESPOON PINK PEARL SPRINKLES
- 1 TABLESPOON WHITE PEARL SPRINKLES

1 Trim edges of cakes; split each cake in half. Secure one cake layer to cake board with a little frosting; spread a third of the frosting over cake, sandwich with another cake layer. Repeat with another third of the frosting and one more cake layer. (Discard or reserve remaining cake for another use). Spread remaining frosting over top of cake.

2 Place heart cutters, one at a time, on frosting. Sprinkle inside of cutter with sprinkles. Use back of a teaspoon to lightly press sprinkles into frosting to secure. Gently lift cutter, being careful not to spread sprinkles outside of heart shape. Repeat with remaining sprinkles to decorate cake with hearts.

TIPS Use any shaped cutter for this cake; try snowflakes or stars. You can use letter cutters and write the name of the birthday child on the cake. Use coloured sprinkles that suit the occasion of your party. If using butter cream instead of strawberry frosting, you will need one quantity of butter cream coloured pale pink (page 327).

TIP

We used white chocolate rocks to decorate the front of the moat.

BRAVE KNIGHTS DEFEND
THE REALM

1 Trim cakes to sit flat. Spread top of one cake with a little frosting; secure other cake on top. Secure to cake board, cut-side down, with a little frosting. Reserve 1 tablespoon of the frosting. Spread remaining frosting all over cake.

2 Cut turret shapes from one short side of four waffles. Secure turret waffles to front and back corners of cake; lay two waffles long-side down in centre at front and back of cake; secure four waffles short-side up, on sides of cake. You will have two waffles left over.

3 Place remaining waffles flat on top of cake in centre; place four wafers on top. Place one wafer in front of pile, as pictured. Place wafer cone on top of one flat-based cone; position on top of wafer pile.

4 Cut rainbow sour strap into flag shapes; thread onto skewers. Place fruit rings on top of remaining flat-based cones; push a skewer through centre of each cone, as pictured. Position cones in corners of castle.

5 Cut red sour straps into window and door shapes. Secure to cake with a little frosting.

6 Cut remaining wafer into a door shape; secure at base of door as a drawbridge.

EQUIPMENT
- 30CM X 40XM (12-INCH X 16-INCH) RECTANGULAR CAKE BOARD (PAGE 332)
- 4 LONG WOODEN SKEWERS

CAKE
- 1 X 450G (14½-OUNCE) PACKET DOUBLE UNFILLED SPONGE SLABS
- ½ X 453G (14½-OUNCE) TUB VANILLA FROSTING

DECORATIONS
- 12 ENGLISH-STYLE WAFFLES
- 6 ICE-CREAM WAFERS
- 1 CONE-SHAPED WAFER CONE
- 5 FLAT-BASED ICE-CREAM CONES
- 1 RAINBOW SOUR STRAP
- 4 RED SOUR FRUIT RINGS
- 1 RED SOUR STRAP

LITTLE BABY
BUNTING

EQUIPMENT

- 30CM (12-INCH) ROUND CAKE BOARD (PAGE 332)

CAKE

- 2 X 600G (1¼-POUND) PACKETS WHITE CHOCOLATE MUD CAKE, ICING REMOVED
- 1 X 453G (14½-OUNCE) TUB STRAWBERRY FROSTING

DECORATIONS

- 3 X 200G (6½-OUNCE) PACKETS MUSK STICKS
- 1½M (60-INCH) MINIATURE BUNTING
- SMALL WOODEN TOOTHPICKS
- 2 X 25CM (10-INCH) PAINTED STICKS

1 Level cake tops. Secure one cake to cake board with a little frosting; spread cake top with ⅓ cup of the frosting. Top with other cake. Spread all over with remaining frosting.

2 Trim musk sticks so they sit 5mm (¼-inch) above cake. Position musk sticks around side of cake. Secure bunting around cake using toothpicks to hold bunting in place.

3 Secure bunting to sticks; push sticks into cake, as pictured.

TIPS Miniature bunting can be found at most craft and party shops or make your own (page 124). For a boy, decorate with green or yellow fruit sticks and matching bunting, or use the colours of his favourite team (of course, this also can be done for girls and their favourite team).

WHIMSICAL MERINGUE CAKE

1 Level tops of cakes to remove icing. Secure one cake to cake board with a little frosting. Spread top of cake with 1/3 cup of the frosting; top with the remaining cake. Spread top and side of cake with remaining frosting.

2 Secure meringues around side and top of cake.

TIPS You can make your own meringues for this cake and colour them any colour you like. If using butter cream instead of vanilla frosting, you will need one quantity of butter cream coloured pale yellow (page 327).

EQUIPMENT

- 25CM (10-INCH) ROUND CAKE BOARD (PAGE 332)

CAKE
- 2 X 600G (1¼-POUND) PACKETS ROUND CHOCOLATE MUD CAKE
- 1 X 453G (14½-OUNCE) TUB VANILLA FROSTING

DECORATIONS
- 2 X 100G (3-OUNCE) PACKETS MINI RAINBOW MERINGUES

HOLD ON TIGHT, WE'RE TAKING FLIGHT

EQUIPMENT
- PAPER PIPING BAG (PAGE 336)
- 30CM (12-INCH) ROUND CAKE BOARD (PAGE 332)

CAKE
- 1 X 453G (14½-OUNCE) TUB VANILLA FROSTING
- BLUE FOOD COLOURING GEL
- 3 X 600G (1¼-POUND) PACKETS ROUND CHOCOLATE CAKE

DECORATIONS
- 1 ROLL GREEN APPLE BUBBLE GUM TAPE
- RABBIT FIGURINE
- 2 YELLOW BOOTLACES
- 3 LARGE FLAT LOLLIPOPS
- 1 LARGE ROUND LOLLIPOP
- 3 SMALL ROUND LOLLIPOPS
- 2 SMALL FLAT LOLLIPOPS

1 Spoon ¼ cup of the frosting into piping bag; reserve. Tint remaining frosting blue.

2 Level cake tops (page 333). Secure one cake, cut-side down, on cake board. Spread top of cake with ¼ cup of the blue frosting. Repeat with remaining two cakes, layering cakes on top of each other. Cover top and side of cake with remaining blue frosting.

3 Using picture as a guide, cut bubble gum tape to make grass. Press grass around bottom edge of cake. Position rabbit figurine onto cake. Position bootlaces and push lollipops into side and top of cake.

4 Pipe clouds onto cake with reserved frosting.

TIPS

We used flat and round lollipops for this cake. If using non-edible decorations, make sure that they are removed before serving.

TIP

Use regular hundreds & thousands for a brighter, less pastel cake.

FAIRY PRINCESS BIRTHDAY CAKE

1 Level cake tops (page 333). Split all cakes in half. Secure one cake half to 20cm cake board. Spread with 1/3 cup of the ganache; top with another cake half. Repeat with ganache and another cake half (so there are three cake halves sandwiched with ganache).

2 Cut 10cm circles from remaining three cake halves. Secure one cake half to 10cm cake board. Spread with ¼ cup of the ganache; top with another cake half. Repeat with ganache and remaining cake half.

3 Pour hundreds & thousands into a shallow oven tray. Spread sides of cakes with ganache. Hold cakes by top and bottom and roll in hundreds & thousands, ensuring that all ganache is covered.

4 Secure larger cake to 30cm (12-inch) cake board with a little ganache. Spread tops of both cakes with ganache; sprinkle remaining hundreds & thousands over cake tops, ensuring that all ganache is covered. Refrigerate 30 minutes or until firm.

5 Carefully spread a little ganache on top of larger cake in centre; place smaller cake on top (this helps to secure two cakes together if it is to be transported). Tie ribbon around base of top cake with a bow.

EQUIPMENT
- 20CM (8-INCH) ROUND CARDBOARD CAKE BOARD
- 10CM (4-INCH) ROUND CUTTER
- 10CM (4-INCH) ROUND CARDBOARD CAKE BOARD
- 30CM (12-INCH) ROUND CAKE BOARD (PAGE 332)

CAKE
- 3 X 600G (1¼-POUND) PACKETS WHITE CHOCOLATE MUD CAKE
- 2 QUANTITIES WHITE CHOCOLATE GANACHE (PAGE 327)

DECORATIONS
- 2 X 190G (6-OUNCE) PACKETS NATURAL COLOURED HUNDREDS & THOUSANDS
- 1½M (60-INCH) X 4CM (1½-INCH) WIDE PINK STRIPED RIBBON

MINTY RASPBERRY ICE-CREAM CAKE

EQUIPMENT

- 18CM (7¼-INCH) (CLOSED BASE MEASUREMENT) ROUND SPRINGFORM PAN
- 25CM (10-INCH) SERVING PLATE OR CAKE STAND

CAKE

- ½ X 460G (14½-OUNCE) PACKAGED DOUBLE UNFILLED SPONGE CAKE ROUNDS
- ⅓ CUP (80ML) STRAWBERRY TOPPING
- 2-LITRES (8-CUPS) VANILLA ICE-CREAM, SOFTENED
- PINK AND GREEN FOOD COLOURING
- ½ CUP (90G) JELLY RASPBERRIES, CHOPPED COARSELY
- ½ CUP (110G) SPEARMINT LEAVES, CHOPPED COARSELY
- ½ X 453G (14½-OUNCE) TUB STRAWBERRY FROSTING

DECORATIONS

- 6 ASSORTED ICING FLOWERS
- 2 SPEARMINT LEAVES, HALVED

1 Line base and sides of pan with plastic wrap, allowing a 5cm (2-inch) overhang.

2 Split cake in half; brush cut sides with strawberry topping. Place one cake half, topping-side up, in base of pan.

3 Divide ice-cream evenly among three bowls. Return two bowls to freezer while working with third bowl.

4 Tint first bowl of ice-cream pink; add raspberries, stir to combine. Spoon over cake; smooth surface. Freeze 20 minutes or until just firm.

5 Remove second bowl of ice-cream from freezer to soften slightly. Spoon vanilla ice-cream over pink ice-cream; smooth surface. Freeze 20 minutes or until just firm.

6 Remove last bowl of ice-cream from freezer to soften slightly. Tint ice-cream green; add chopped spearmint leaves, stir to combine. Spoon over vanilla ice-cream; smooth surface. Top with remaining cake layer, topping-side down.

7 Loosely cover ice-cream cake with plastic wrap. Freeze 4 hours or overnight until firm. Remove from pan; place on serving plate. Spread frosting over cake top; decorate with flowers and halved spearmint leaves.

TIPS You only need one round sponge for this recipe. Remove each bowl from the freezer for 5 minutes before you are ready to use it to soften the ice-cream slightly. You could buy a tub of neapolitan ice-cream and divide the flavours into separate bowls to soften; add the mint leaves to the chocolate ice-cream for a choc-mint flavour. Make this cake the day before the party to allow the ice-cream layers time to set.

TIPS
Use cake pans as a guide to draw and cut the circles. Before adding the rabbit's head, fill the hole in the hat with lollies, allowing them to flow over the top.

ABRACADABRA THE
RABBIT

1 Level cake tops (page 333). Secure one cake, cut-side down, on cake board; spread top with ¼ cup of the chocolate frosting. Top with a second cake; spread top with ¼ cup of the frosting. Using 11.5cm cutter, cut a circle from centre of remaining cake; discard circle. Place cake ring on top of cake stack. Spread chocolate frosting over top, sides and around hole inside cake.

2 Melt chocolate (page 337). Mark a 22cm (8¾-inch) circle on a sheet of baking paper; turn paper over. Spread chocolate on paper to make a circle. Stand 5 minutes or until just set. Using 10.5cm cutter, cut a circle from centre of chocolate. Stand 5 minutes or until chocolate has set hard. When chocolate is ready, remove smaller circle and place inside hole. Using picture as a guide, attach chocolate ring to cake to make a hat rim.

3 Using a small pair of scissors, cut ear shapes from wafers. Spread one side of wafer with vanilla frosting then sprinkle with coconut; repeat with other wafer. Spread muffin top with a little vanilla frosting; sprinkle with coconut. Place muffin in hat; position wafers as ears. Attach double D lollies as eyes. Thinly slice 2 rounds from licorice; attach to eyes. Trim another piece of licorice into a nose shape; position on rabbit's face.

4 Roll ready-made white icing on a surface dusted with a little sifted icing sugar; cut out gloves using template (page 339). Attach jelly bean slice to gloves for button. Position gloves over side of hat, and wand at base of cake.

EQUIPMENT

- 30CM (12-INCH) ROUND CAKE BOARD (PAGE 332)
- 10.5CM (4-INCH) AND 11.5CM (4½-INCH) ROUND CUTTERS

CAKE

- 3 X 600G (1¼-POUND) PACKAGED ROUND CHOCOLATE CAKES
- 1 X 453G (14½-OUNCE) TUB DARK CHOCOLATE FROSTING
- ½ X 453G (14½-OUNCE) TUB VANILLA FROSTING

DECORATIONS

- 1⅓ CUPS (200G) DARK CHOCOLATE MELTS
- 2 PLAIN ICE-CREAM WAFERS
- 2 TABLESPOONS DESICCATED COCONUT
- 1 CHOC-CHIP MUFFIN
- 2 SUGAR-FREE DOUBLE D ORANGE JELLY ROUNDS
- SMALL PIECE ROUND SOFT-EATING LICORICE
- 150G (4½ OUNCES) READY-MADE WHITE ICING (PAGE 327)
- PURE ICING (CONFECTIONERS') SUGAR, FOR DUSTING
- 1 BLACK JELLY BEAN, SLICED THINLY
- MAGIC WAND

FAERIES OF THE GLEN TERRARIUM

EQUIPMENT

- SMALL AQUARIUM OR STRAIGHT-SIDED GLASS SERVING DISH

CAKE

- 6 CUPS (530G) CHOCOLATE CAKE CRUMBS (SEE TIPS)
- 2 TABLESPOONS READY-MADE VANILLA FROSTING
- 1 MINI VANILLA CUPCAKE

DECORATIONS

- 2 CUPS (160G) DESICCATED COCONUT
- GREEN FOOD COLOURING
- 50G (1½ OUNCES) WHITE CHOCOLATE MELTS
- 200G (6½-OUNCE) PACKET SPEARMINT LEAVES, HALVED
- 12 RED MINI M&M'S
- 200G (6½ OUNCES) DARK CHOCOLATE MELTS
- 6 GREEN LOLLIPOPS, CRUSHED
- 4 WHITE MILK BOTTLES
- 3 RED M&M'S
- MINI HOUSE AND FAIRIES, TO DECORATE

1 Using picture as a guide, spread cake crumbs over base of aquarium.

2 Tint the coconut green (page 336); sprinkle over cake crumbs.

3 Reserve four white chocolate Melts. Melt remaining white chocolate (page 337). Decorate wall of aquarium with some spearmint leaves to make trees. Secure with melted chocolate.

4 Spread frosting over cupcake. Decorate with mini M&M's.

5 Melt the dark chocolate (page 337). Using picture as a guide, pipe chocolate onto baking paper to make a tall and a short tree. Sprinkle tops of trees with crushed lollipops. Allow to set.

6 Trim top off milk bottles. Secure a reserved white chocolate melt on top of each bottle to make toadstools.

7 Gently push trees into cake crumbs. Using picture as a guide, position toadstools, cupcake, remaining lollies, and decorations.

TIPS We crumbled 2 x 600g (1¼-pound) packets chocolate cake to make the cake crumbs. Remove any non-edible decorations before serving.

HAT CUPCAKES

WIZARD HAT

Melt 300g (9½ ounces) white chocolate Melts (page 337). Tint with purple colouring suitable for chocolate. Dip 12 mini waffle ice-cream cones into chocolate. Sprinkle with combined purple and gold sprinkles. Allow to set. Tint half a 453g (14½-ounce) tub vanilla frosting purple. Spoon frosting into a piping bag fitted with a 1.5cm (¾-inch) plain tube; pipe frosting onto 12 cupcakes. Top cupcakes with cones. Decorate with gold stars, as pictured.

CLOWN HAT

Melt 150g (6 ounces) white chocolate Melts (page 337). Tint with yellow colouring suitable for chocolate. Dip 12 mini waffle ice-cream cones in yellow chocolate to cover half the cone. Allow to set. Melt another 150g (6 ounces) white chocolate Melts. Tint with blue colouring suitable for chocolate. Dip remaining half of cones in blue chocolate. Allow to set. Tint half a 453g (14½-ounce) tub vanilla frosting red. Spoon frosting into a piping bag fitted with a 1.5cm (¾-inch) plain tube; pipe frosting onto 12 cupcakes. Top cupcakes with cones. Decorate cones with Jaffas and sliced white mini marshmallows, securing with a little melted chocolate.

ELF HAT

Melt 300g (9½ ounces) white chocolate Melts
(page 337). Tint with green colouring suitable
for chocolate. Dip 12 mini waffle ice-cream
cones in chocolate. Allow to set. Tint half a
453g (14½-ounce) tub vanilla frosting yellow.
Spoon frosting into a piping bag fitted with a
1.5cm (¾-inch) plain tube; pipe frosting onto
12 cupcakes. Top cupcakes with cone. Cut
12 x 17cm (6¾in) strips from green apple
bubble gum tape. Using picture as a guide,
cut one side of each strip into 5mm triangles
to form a crown. Position crowns around cones,
trim and secure with a little melted chocolate.
Decorate crowns with yellow sugar pearls.
Top cones with a yellow M&M, securing
with a little melted chocolate.

PRINCESS HAT

Melt 300g (9½ ounces) white chocolate Melts
(page 337). Tint with pink colouring suitable
for chocolate. Dip 12 mini waffle ice-cream
cones into chocolate. Sprinkle with pink
sanding sugar. Allow to set. Tint half a 453g
(14½-ounce) tub vanilla frosting pink. Spoon
vanilla frosting into a piping bag fitted with a
1.5cm (¾-inch) plain tube; pipe frosting onto
12 cupcakes. Top cupcakes with cones. Spoon
pink frosting into a piping bag fitted with
a 5mm (¼-inch) fluted tube. Pipe around
cone. Decorate with candied flowers
and pink and white sugar pearls.

COLOUR ME IN

Using the coloured doughnuts as a guide, colour in the other doughnuts however you like. Be sure to make the sprinkles bold and bright.

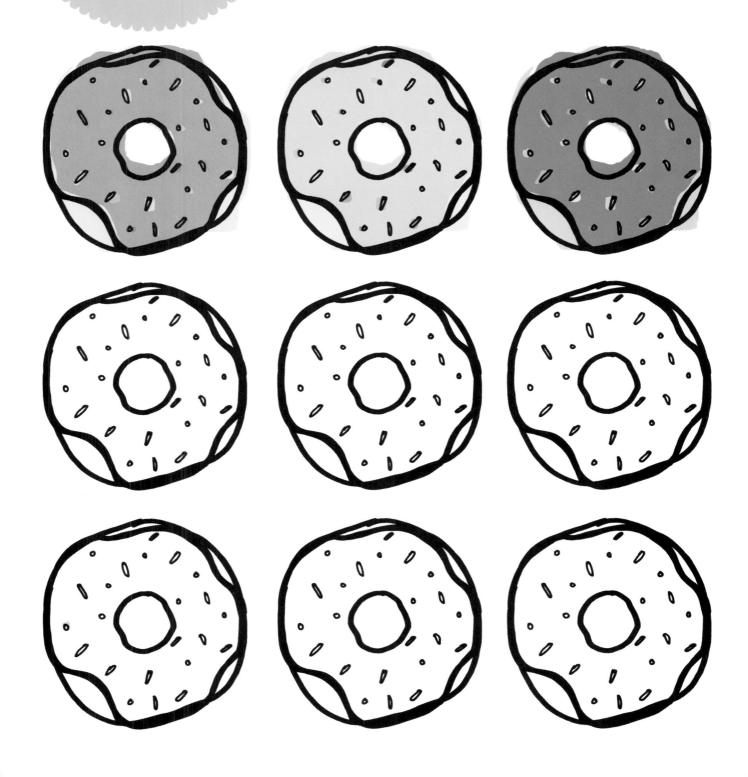

PAPER
ICE BLOCKS

Make your own ice-blocks! Photocopy and cut the templates out then glue them onto a ice-block stick.

CUT   CUT   CUT

CUT   CUT   CUT

Tips & Techniques

CAKE RECIPES

IF YOU WANT TO MAKE YOUR OWN CAKES, THESE RECIPES WILL ALL BAKE AT SIMILAR TEMPERATURES, TIMES, AND IN THE SAME PAN SIZES AS THE PACKET MIX CAKES SUGGESTED IN EACH RECIPE. ONE QUANTITY OF EACH OF THESE CAKE RECIPES IS EQUIVALENT TO ONE 470G (15-OUNCE) PACKAGED CAKE MIX.

BASIC BUTTER CAKE

- 125G (4 OUNCES) BUTTER, SOFTENED
- ½ TEASPOON VANILLA EXTRACT
- ¾ CUP (165G) CASTER (SUPERFINE) SUGAR
- 2 EGGS
- 1½ CUPS (225G) SELF-RAISING FLOUR
- ½ CUP (125ML) MILK

Preheat oven. Grease (and line) pan(s). Beat butter, extract and sugar in a small bowl with an electric mixer until light and fluffy. Beat in eggs, one at a time. Stir in sifted flour and milk, in two batches. Bake as directed. To marble a butter cake, place portions of cake mixture in three bowls then tint each with different colours. Drop spoonfuls of mixture into pan(s), alternating colours, then swirl together with a skewer.

CHOCOLATE CAKE

- 1⅓ CUPS (200G) SELF-RAISING FLOUR
- ½ CUP (50G) COCOA POWDER
- 125G (4 OUNCES) BUTTER, SOFTENED
- ½ TEASPOON VANILLA EXTRACT
- 1¼ CUPS (275G) CASTER (SUPERFINE) SUGAR
- 2 EGGS
- ⅔ CUP (160ML) WATER

Preheat oven. Grease (and line) pan(s). Sift flour and cocoa into a medium bowl, add remaining ingredients; beat on low speed with an electric mixer until ingredients are combined. Increase speed to medium; beat for 3 minutes or until mixture is smooth and changed to a lighter colour. Bake as directed.

DARK CHOCOLATE MUD CAKE

- 225G (7 OUNCES) BUTTER, CHOPPED
- 360G (11½ OUNCES) DARK CHOCOLATE, CHOPPED COARSELY
- ¾ CUP (165G) FIRMLY PACKED BROWN SUGAR
- ¾ CUP (180ML) WATER
- 1 CUP (150G) PLAIN (ALL-PURPOSE) FLOUR
- ¼ CUP (35G) SELF-RAISING FLOUR
- 2 TABLESPOONS COCOA POWDER
- 2 EGGS

Preheat oven. Grease (and line) pan(s). Combine butter, chocolate, sugar and the water in a medium saucepan; stir over low heat until smooth. Cool 30 minutes. Whisk in sifted flours and cocoa then eggs. Bake as directed.

WHITE CHOCOLATE MUD CAKE

- 165G (5 OUNCES) BUTTER, CHOPPED
- 100G (3 OUNCES) WHITE CHOCOLATE, CHOPPED COARSELY
- 1⅓ CUPS (295G) CASTER (SUPERFINE) SUGAR
- ⅔ CUP (160ML) MILK
- 1 CUP (150G) PLAIN (ALL-PURPOSE) FLOUR
- ⅓ CUP (50G) SELF-RAISING FLOUR
- 1 EGG

Preheat oven. Grease (and line) pan(s). Combine butter, chocolate, sugar and milk in a medium saucepan; stir over low heat until smooth. Cool 30 minutes. Whisk in sifted flours, then egg. Bake as directed.

GLUTEN-FREE BUTTER CAKE

- 100G (3 OUNCES) BUTTER, SOFTENED
- 1 CUP (150G) GLUTEN-FREE SELF-RAISING FLOUR
- ½ CUP (110G) CASTER (SUPERFINE) SUGAR
- ¼ CUP (60ML) MILK
- 1 EGG
- 1 EGG WHITE

Preheat oven. Grease (and line) pan(s). Beat butter in a small bowl with an electric mixer until changed to a paler colour. Sift flour and 2 tablespoons of the sugar together. Beat flour mixture and milk into butter, in two batches, until combined. Beat egg and egg white in a small bowl with an electric mixer until thick and creamy. Gradually add remaining sugar, beating until sugar dissolves. Gradually pour egg mixture into flour mixture with motor operating on a low speed; beat only until combined. Bake as directed.

GLUTEN-FREE CARROT CAKE

- 1 CUP (125G) SOY OR BESAN (CHICKPEA) FLOUR
- ¾ CUP (110G) 100% CORN CORNFLOUR (CORNSTARCH)
- 2 TEASPOONS GLUTEN-FREE BAKING POWDER
- 1 TEASPOON BICARBONATE OF SODA (BAKING SODA)
- 2 TEASPOONS MIXED SPICE
- 1 CUP (220G) FIRMLY PACKED BROWN SUGAR
- 1 CUP (120G) COARSELY CHOPPED ROASTED WALNUTS
- 1½ CUPS (360G) FIRMLY PACKED COARSELY GRATED CARROT
- ½ CUP (125ML) EXTRA LIGHT OLIVE OIL
- ½ CUP (120G) SOUR CREAM
- 3 EGGS

Preheat oven. Grease (and line) pan(s). Sift flour, cornflour, baking powder, soda and spice into a large bowl; stir in sugar, walnuts and carrot. Stir in combined oil, sour cream and eggs. Bake as directed.

ICING RECIPES

BUTTER CREAM

Basic butter cream is also called vienna cream; the flavour can be varied by adding any extract or essence you like.

- 125G (4 OUNCES) UNSALTED BUTTER, SOFTENED
- 1½ CUPS (240G) ICING (CONFECTIONERS') SUGAR
- 2 TABLESPOONS MILK

Beat butter in a small bowl with an electric mixer until as white as possible. Gradually beat in half the sifted sugar, milk, then remaining sugar. To make chocolate butter cream, sift ⅓ cup (35g) cocoa powder in with first batch of icing sugar.

GLACÉ ICING

- 2¼ CUPS (360G) ICING (CONFECTIONERS') SUGAR
- ¼ CUP (60ML) WATER, APPROXIMATELY
- FOOD COLOURING

Sift sugar into a medium heatproof bowl, stir in enough of the water to give a firm paste. Colour as desired. Stir paste over a medium saucepan of hot water (the water should not touch the bottom of bowl) until icing is spreadable; do not overheat. The bottom of the bowl should feel warm (not hot) to the touch. Use immediately. (Also see page 337.)

ROYAL ICING

- 1½ CUPS (240G) PURE ICING (CONFECTIONERS') SUGAR
- 1 EGG WHITE
- ½ TEASPOON LEMON JUICE

Sift sugar through a very fine sieve. Lightly beat egg white in a small bowl with an electric mixer; add sifted sugar, a tablespoon at a time. When icing reaches firm peaks, use a wooden spoon to beat in juice. Royal icing must be kept covered, either with a well wrung out wet cloth then plastic wrap, or with plastic wrap pressed onto surface of icing. Royal icing develops a crust when it's left open to the air – this usually makes the icing unusable, particularly for piping.

READY-MADE WHITE ICING

Ready-made icing is available from cake-decorating suppliers and supermarkets. There are several brands available and they are very easy to use. Break off as much icing as you need; re-wrap remaining icing to exclude the air or a crust will develop, which will spoil the smooth texture of the icing. Knead the piece of icing on a surface lightly dusted with sifted icing sugar. If colouring the icing, start working tiny amounts of the colouring through the icing. The icing should be smooth and free from stickiness. Only work with small amounts of icing at a time as the air will dry it out. Cover any rolled-out icing with plastic wrap. To cover a cake with ready-made icing, follow the steps on page 334.

GANACHE

Ganache is a mixture of melted chocolate and cream. It is wonderfully simple to make and versatile to use. It can be used while it's still warm as a glaze over a cake. Or let the ganache partly set, either at a cool room temperature or in the refrigerator, then beat it with a wooden spoon until it's spreadable – making it a perfect filling or frosting.

Ganache can be refrigerated for around 30 minutes, or until it becomes thick and spreadable, then whipped with an electric mixer until it increases in volume and becomes fluffy, making it ideal for a frosting or filling. Ganache will keep in the refrigerator, covered tightly, for about two weeks (stand at room temperature to soften before use), or frozen for 3 months; thaw overnight in the refrigerator, or thaw it in the microwave oven, using short bursts of power.

DARK OR MILK CHOCOLATE GANACHE

- ½ CUP (125ML) POURING CREAM
- 200G (6½ OUNCES) MILK OR DARK CHOCOLATE, BROKEN INTO PIECES

Bring cream to the boil in a small saucepan; remove from heat. Add chocolate to pan with hot cream; stir until smooth. Cool mixture to room temperature before beating or whipping ganache to desired consistency.

WHITE CHOCOLATE GANACHE

- 360G (11½ OUNCES) WHITE CHOCOLATE, BROKEN INTO PIECES
- ½ CUP (125ML) POURING CREAM

Process chocolate until finely chopped. Bring cream to the boil in a small saucepan; remove from heat. Add chocolate to pan with hot cream; stir until smooth. Cool mixture to room temperature before beating or whipping ganache to desired consistency.

BAKING INFORMATION

CAKE PANS

There's a vast array of cake pans available from chain stores, supermarkets, cookware and homeware shops, and also from shops that specialise in cake decorating supplies. Price is a guide to quality when it comes to cake pans; if you buy wisely and look after the pans, they should last a lifetime. Cake pans are made from many different materials – uncoated aluminium, which is our favourite, are becoming increasingly difficult to find. There are metal pans with non-stick coating, which still need greasing, scratch easily and tend to make baked goods develop a heavy crust (decrease the oven temperature to compensate for this). Heavy good-quality tin pans bake cakes well, but usually work better if the goods are baked at a slightly lower temperature than

normal. Inexpensive cake pans made from thin flimsy tin are not a good investment as they tend to twist and buckle, often after the first time they're used. Silicone pans are also available; cakes baked in these develop a light crust, which is sometimes a good thing. Muffins and cupcakes work particularly well in these pans.

PACKET OR HOME MADE CAKES

Unbaked cake mixtures (both packet and homemade) will tolerate standing at a cool room temperature for at least an hour before baking. We have used cakes made from packet mixes throughout this book for consistency of size and baking times. If you want to make your own cakes, choose any of the recipes on page 326; they will all bake at similar temperatures, times, and in the same pan sizes as the packet

mix cakes suggested in each recipe. One quantity of any of the cake recipes is equivalent to one 470g packaged cake mix.

BEATING PACKET MIXES

It's important to beat packet mixes properly using an electric mixer – not a food processor or blender. We found a stand (bench) mixer gave us the best results, simply because it's easier to let the machine do the work rather than holding a hand-held mixer (there is a tendency to under-beat the mixture using one of these). Also, it's important to beat the packet mixes enough to develop the volume of the mixture. Have the ingredients to be added at room temperature for the best results, start the mixer at a low speed to incorporate the ingredients, then gradually increase the speed to medium. As a rule, one packet

of cake mix fits into a small bowl, two or three packets into a medium bowl, and four packets into a large bowl. The beaters should always be well down in the mixture to create volume.

BAKING

The oven temperatures in this book are for conventional ovens; for fan-forced ovens, decrease the temperature by 10-20 degrees. Fan-forced ovens should bake everything that is being cooked in the oven evenly, however, some domestic ovens have hot spots. If you need to bake cakes on two oven racks, it will be necessary to change the positions of the cakes about halfway through the baking time. It's fine to cook more than one cake on the same rack, but the cake pans shouldn't touch each other, the sides of the oven or the closed oven door. It's usually a good idea to change the positions of the cake

pans on the same rack, too. Allow for the cake to rise when positioning racks before the oven is preheated. As a guide, cakes should be baked in the centre of the oven, towards the lower half of the oven. If the oven is loaded with cakes of varying sizes, they might take a little longer to bake than our recipes indicate.

MEASURING CAKE QUANTITIES

To achieve the same results as we did for the cakes in this book, it's important to measure the mixture accurately into the correct-sized cake pans. Often there is some cake mixture left over, just use it to make cupcakes for the party. Some of the cakes in this book require half-packets of cake mixture to be used; make the whole cake then use half the mixture, as indicated by the recipe, and use the remaining mixture to make additional patty or cupcakes for the party.

FOOD COLOURINGS

Use good-quality colourings for the best results; they will 'hold' the colour in the icing. Some of the inexpensive liquid colourings will fade or darken the icing on standing. Icings or frostings based on butter are the most difficult to colour as butter is yellow, so any colour will be affected by the base colour. This is why it's important to beat the butter until it's as white as possible. We found unsalted butter to work (and taste) the best. Fluffy frosting and royal icing are the easiest to colour, because they're white to begin with. Coloured icings can change on standing, particularly if you're using liquid colourings. If possible (it's not with fluffy frosting), colour a small portion of the icing to the shade you want, keep it airtight, and let it stand for a few hours before colouring the whole batch.

PANS AND EQUIPMENT

1. DEEP ROUND CAKE PANS

Use pans made from aluminium or good-quality tin. Cake pans that have a non-stick coating can be used, but cakes baked in these pans should be baked at a slightly lower temperature than those baked in aluminium or good-quality tin pans.

2. CHOCOLATE MOULDS, ICE-CREAM SCOOP AND CANDY THERMOMETER

We used plastic chocolate moulds, there are many types available – all good. A candy thermometer is handy to have in the kitchen as it takes the guess-work out of making sure sugar syrups reach the correct temperature.

3. CUTTERS

We used a variety of different-sized and -shaped metal cutters in this book. Plastic cutters can be used, but they don't cut as neatly as those made from metal.

4. SWISS ROLL PAN

Choose a straight-sided metal dish that has a solid flat base. Trim the cake's corners and sides if necessary before cutting into the shape required. A baking pan is a similar shape to a swiss roll pan, however, its sides are at least 5cm (2 inches) in height, or more.

5. LOAF PAN AND NUT ROLL TINS

Loaf pans come in a wide variety of sizes and are made from many different materials. Nut roll tins are made from tin and are available from cookware shops.

6. PATTY AND MUFFIN PANS

There are many shapes and sizes available in cookware shops department stores, supermarkets etc. The pans are made from a variety of materials, including those with a non-stick coating, aluminium, tin and silicone.

7. PIPING BAGS AND TUBES

Plastic piping bags and tubes are available from supermarkets; fabric piping bags are available from cookware shops and cake decorating suppliers. Piping tubes are available in plastic and metal, in a wide variety of shapes and sizes.

8. SAVARIN PAN

These are available from specialty cookware shops and are made from aluminium. They are available in a number of sizes.

9. DOLLY VARDEN PAN AND METAL PUDDING STEAMER

Both are made from aluminium. Cakes made in these pans need to be baked at a lower than normal oven temperature to make sure the cake mixtures cook through in the centre.

10. DEEP SQUARE CAKE PANS

We used pans made from aluminium or good-quality tin. Some cakes look better if they're baked in sharp-cornered pans such as those pictured. Tin conducts oven heat quickly, so bake cakes at a slightly lower temperature than if using an aluminium cake pan.

11. PATTY CASES

A wide variety of colours, patterns and sizes are available from supermarkets, cookware shops, chain stores and cake decorating suppliers. They can be made from paper in varying thicknesses and quality, also from foil and silicone.

12. SKEWERS, STRAWS AND FLORISTS' WIRE

Florists' wire is used for supporting shapes made from icing, it is available from craft shops and cake decorating suppliers. Wooden skewers and strong plastic straws can be used for supporting cake tiers, trim them to the correct length.

1.

2.

3.

4.

5.

6.

7.

8.

9.

10.

11.

12.

STEP BY STEP

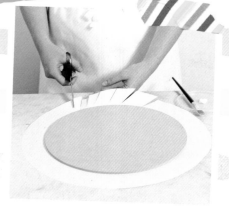

COVERING A SQUARE CAKE BOARD

Cut the covering paper about 5cm (2 inches) larger than the board, place the board, top-side down on the back of the paper. Use tape or glue to stick the paper to the board. If the paper is thick, cut the corners out of the paper as if covering a book.

COVERING A ROUND CAKE BOARD

Cut the covering paper about 5cm (2 inches) larger than the board, place the board, top-side down on the back of the paper. Snip the paper border, on an angle, all the way around. Fold each snipped piece of paper over onto the board; tape or glue the paper onto the board.

GREASING CAKE PANS

Melted butter, applied evenly with a pastry brush, is the best method for greasing a cake pan, particularly those cake pans that are patterned, or are of an unusual shape.

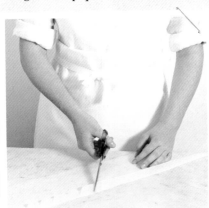

FLOURING A GREASED CAKE PAN

We have indicated when to grease and flour cake pans. Refrigerate the greased pan for a few minutes to set the butter. Sprinkle the buttered area with flour, turn and tap the pan until the pan is floured evenly, then tap the pan over the sink or bin, to get rid of the excess flour.

LINING A ROUND CAKE PAN

Cut a strip of baking paper, long enough to encircle the inside of the pan and overlap slightly plus about an extra 7cm (2¾ inches) to allow for the fold over at the base of the pan and for the paper to extend above the side of the pan. Fold about 2cm (¾-inch) of the paper over,

then snip the paper, on an angle up to the fold. Lightly grease the inside of the pan to hold the lining paper in place, position the snipped paper around the side of the pan. Using the base of the pan as a guide, trace around the base of the pan. Cut out the round of paper, cutting slightly inside the marked circle. Position the paper in the pan.

LINING A RECTANGULAR OR SQUARE CAKE PAN

Cut strips of baking paper long enough to cover base and sides of the lightly greased cake pan, sometimes only one strip of paper is necessary. Always extend the paper over the sides of the pan by about 5cm (2 inches).

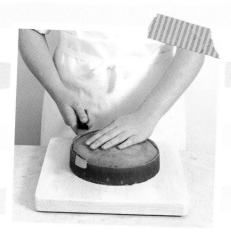

LEVELLING CAKES

Most cakes need to have their tops cut off to make the cakes sit flat on a cake board or plate. Use a large sharp serrated knife to do this.

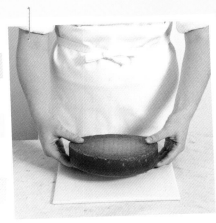

PREPARING CAKES FOR DECORATING

Most of the cakes in this book are turned top-side down for decorating. There are just a few decorated top-side up, for a domed effect. Recipes will indicate when to position the cake on a cake board or plate.

USING TEMPLATES

If a template is required, trace the template from pages 338-339 onto paper and cut out the shape. Secure the pattern to the cake – usually the bottom of the cake – with toothpicks to hold the pattern firmly in place.

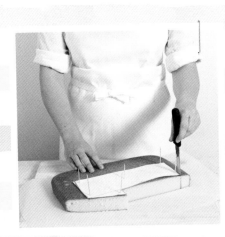

CUTTING OUT THE CAKE

Once the template is in place, use a small sharp, pointed serrated knife to cut carefully around the pattern. Hold the knife upright to get the neatest results.

BRUSHING THE CAKE WITH JAM

Use warmed, sieved jam to brush over the surface of the cake, when recipes indicate this is necessary. Be particular about brushing the jam evenly and thoroughly over any cut surfaces on the cake. If the cake is fresh and crumbly, freeze it for an hour or so to make the job easier.

ROLLING OUT READY-MADE ICING

Use a rolling pin to roll the icing to the correct size and thickness. Roll icing on a surface lightly dusted with a little sifted icing sugar. Use the rolling pin to lift the icing over the cake.

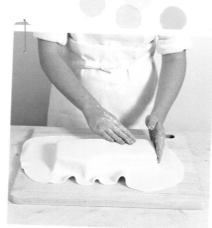

SMOOTHING READY-MADE ICING

Using hands dusted with a little icing sugar, gently mould and smooth the icing around the shape of the cake. Make sure the icing feels like it is clinging to the jam on the cake.

TRIMMING READY-MADE ICING

Use a small sharp pointed knife to carefully trim away the excess icing from around the edge of the cake. Scraps of icing will keep well for months if they're wrapped tightly in plastic wrap to exclude the air.

COLOURING READY-MADE ICING

Use good-quality food colourings for best results. Always start with a tiny dab of the colouring, and work it through the icing with your fingers. Determine the depth and strength of the colouring before adding any more.

CUTTING SHAPES FROM READY-MADE ICING

Use a rolling pin to roll the icing to the correct thickness on a surface dusted with a little sifted icing sugar. Use sharp cutters to cut out shapes. Dry shapes on baking paper until firm, or apply directly to the icing on the cake while still soft.

MAKING FLUFFY MOCK CREAM

Beat the softened butter in a small bowl – make sure that the beaters are well down into the butter – until the butter is as white as possible.

APPLYING THE FINAL COAT OF BUTTER CREAM

Spread the final layer of butter cream evenly over the 'undercoat'. If the cake feels firm, skip the undercoat and simply apply the final layer of butter cream to the cake.

COLOURING BUTTER CREAM

Use a skewer to dab a tiny amount of colouring onto the butter cream, mix the colouring through the butter cream thoroughly before adding any more.

PREPARING CAKE FOR DECORATING

If the cake is very fresh, freeze it for a few hours, or refrigerate it overnight. Using a metal spatula, apply a very thin layer of butter cream evenly over the cold cake; if necessary, refrigerate or freeze the cake to set the 'undercoat'.

ADDING SYRUP TO FLUFFY MOCK CREAM

Gradually add the room temperature syrup in a thin steady stream to the butter while the motor is operating.

MAKING FLUFFY FROSTING

Beat the egg whites until stiff towards the end of the syrup's cooking time; keep beating the egg whites while the syrup reaches the correct temperature. Gradually add the hot syrup to the beating egg whites in a thin steady stream. Beat the frosting until firm peaks form.

COLOURING FLUFFY FROSTING

This frosting should be coloured by beating the colouring into the frosting just before the frosting is to be used. This frosting does not stand well, it should be made and used quite quickly, as it sets on standing.

MAKING A PAPER PIPING BAG

Cut a square from a sheet of baking paper, fold it in half diagonally, then cut it in half along the fold to make two triangles.

SHAPING A PAPER PIPING BAG

Hold the apex of the triangle towards you, wrap one point of the triangle around to form a cone shape, then wrap the other point around; wriggle the three points of the triangle until they line up perfectly.

SECURING A PAPER PIPING BAG

Staple the piping bag so that the staple holds the three points of the triangle in place. Half-fill the bag with icing, snip a tiny piece from the point of the bag, pipe a little icing to judge if the hole is large enough, if not, snip more paper from the point of the bag.

COLOURING COCONUT

Use disposable gloves to stop the colouring staining your skin. Place the coconut into a bowl and rub drops of colouring through the coconut until it's evenly coloured. This method can be used to colour sugar too.

COLOURING SUGAR

Place the sugar into a strong resealable plastic bag; add a little food colouring. Massage the colouring through the sugar until it's evenly coloured. This method can be used to colour coconut too.

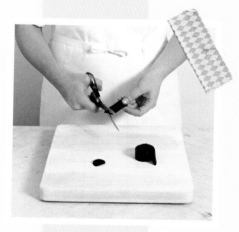

USING LICORICE

Use sharp scissors for cutting and trimming licorice into various shapes and sizes.

MAKING GLACE ICING

Stir the icing over hot water until it's smooth and pourable. The icing must only ever be warm, not hot. Pour the warmed icing over the cake as quickly as possible, preferably without trying to spread it out with a spatula. The icing can be trimmed at the base after it has set.

MELTING CHOCOLATE

Melt chocolate over hot water, it's important that the water in the pan doesn't touch the bottom of the bowl, so that the chocolate doesn't overheat and spoil.

PIPING CHOCOLATE DISCS

Half-fill a paper piping bag with melted chocolate; pipe discs of chocolate onto a baking-paper-lined tray. Tap the tray on the bench to make the chocolate spread slightly, then leave the discs to set at room temperature.

BACKING RIBBON

Sometimes ribbon needs to be backed, so that it doesn't become stained by the icing it's in contact with. Use a strip of adhesive tape the same width as the ribbon, and apply to the back of the ribbon. You might need help to keep the ribbon straight while doing this.

POSITIONING SKEWERS FOR TIERED CAKES

The skewers are needed to support the weight of the top cake. Place the top cake on a cake board. Insert the skewers into the bottom cake, through to the cake board. Mark the height of the skewers; remove them, then trim them so they are level with the top of the bottom cake. Position skewers in the cake.

POSITIONING THE TOP CAKE TIER

Carefully sit the top tier on the skewers. There will be a small gap between the two cakes, cover this with icing or decorations. Remove the top tier, using a metal spatula, before cutting the cakes. Remove the skewers before cutting and serving the cake.

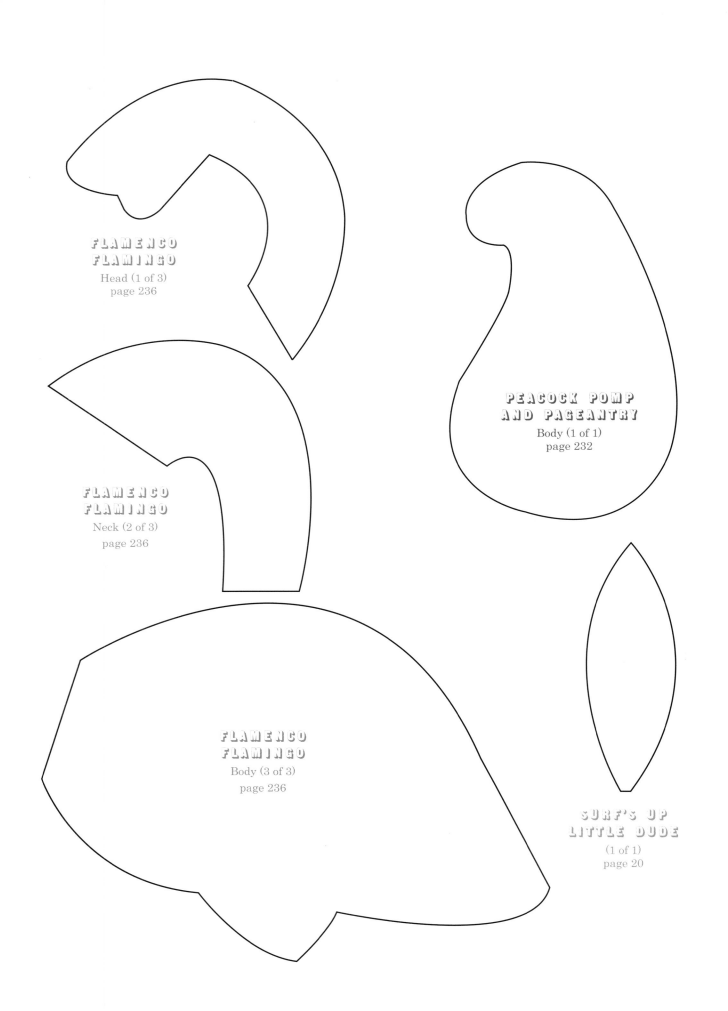

FLAMENCO
FLAMINGO
Head (1 of 3)
page 236

PEACOCK POMP
AND PAGEANTRY
Body (1 of 1)
page 232

FLAMENCO
FLAMINGO
Neck (2 of 3)
page 236

FLAMENCO
FLAMINGO
Body (3 of 3)
page 236

SURF'S UP
LITTLE DUDE
(1 of 1)
page 20

CAKE TEMPLATES

All these patterns are at half size

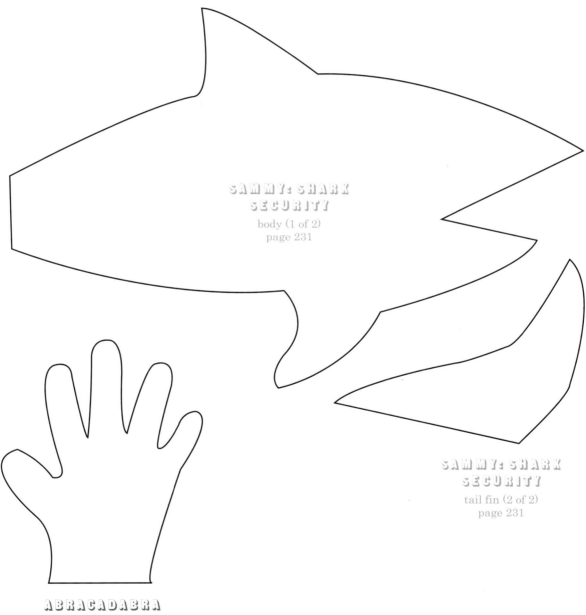

SAMMY: SHARK
SECURITY
body (1 of 2)
page 231

SAMMY: SHARK
SECURITY
tail fin (2 of 2)
page 231

ABRACADABRA
THE RABBIT
glove (1 of 1)
page 317

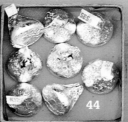

LOLLIES

1. CHOCOLATE RIPPLE BISCUITS
2. FURRY FRIENDS SLAB
3. CURLY WURLY 4. RAINBOW SOUR STRAPS 5. DARK EATING CHOCOLATE 6. MILK EATING CHOCOLATE 7-9. DARK, MILK AND WHITE BUTTONS
10. WAGON WHEEL 11-12. JELLY BEANS 13. RAINBOW NERD ROPE 14-15. CHOCOLATE-COATED PEANUTS AND SULTANAS
16. FLAKE BAR 17-18. RAINBOW AND CHOCOLATE SPRINKLES
19. SILVER CACHOUS 20. GREEN SPRINKLES 21. FRUIT ROLL-UPS
22. WINE GUMS 23-24. BLUE AND ORANGE SPRINKLES 25. TIC TACS
26. MILK BOTTLES 27. MENTOS MINTS 28. HUNDREDS AND THOUSANDS 29. FRUIT & COLA WHEELS 30. JOLS FOREST BERRIES PASTILLES 31. LIQUORICE ALLSORTS 32. METALLIC CACHOUS
33. YELLOW AND WHITE SUGAR PEARLS 34. ICING FLOWERS

35. SPEARMINT LEAVES
36. JELLY SNAKES 37. MINI TOBLERONE BAR 38-39. MINI CHOCOLATE CHIPS 40. M&MS
41. CANDY LETTERS
42. CHOCOLATE-COATED HONEYCOMB 43. SOUR STRAPS
44. HERSHEY'S KISSES
45. LICORICE STRAP 46. BLACK LICORICE (SMOOTH) 47. GREEN APPLE TANG LIQUORICE
48. STRAWBERRY LIQUORICE BITES
49. GUMBALLS 50. MINI MUSKS
51. SOUR WORMS 52. NOODLE SNACK PACK 53. MILO DUOS
54. SMARTIES 55. RAINBOW CHOC DROPS 56. CHOC ROCKS
57. RASPBERRIES 58. CANDIED SUGAR HEART 59. ICING BUTTERFLY 60. ICING FLOWERS
61. JELLY TOTS 62. JUBES
63. FRUIT JELLY RINGS 64. MILO POWDER 65. BUTTERFLY SPRINKLES 66. KOOL MINTS
67. MILK ARROWROOT BISCUITS

68-72. LOLLIPOPS
73. ROCK CANDY 74. SEA SHELL CHOCOLATES 75. POPCORN
76. ESKIMO SNOWBALLS
77. GIANT MARSHMALLOWS
78. MARSHMALLOW POLES
79. MARSHMALLOWS
80. MALLOW BAKES 81. LARGE MARSHMALLOWS 82. SPONGE FINGER BISCUITS 83. FIZZERS
84. COLOURED SUGAR-COATED ALMONDS 85. FROOT LOOPS CEREAL
86. SIXLETS
87. WATERMELON LOLLIES
88. BO-PEEP LOLLIES 89. COLA METEORITES 90. FRUIT STICKS
91. MIXED BERRIES 92. HONEY JUMBLE BISCUITS 93. REGULAR AND MINI OREO BISCUITS
94. MINT PATTIE BISCUITS
95. LARGE RAINBOW SHERBET STRAWS 96. CANDY SNAP SHAPES
97. BRACELET CANDY
98. CANDY CANES 99. SMALL FOIL-COVERED CHOCOLATE SPORTS BALLS
100. CHIP STRAWS 101. POTATO CHIPS 102. LOVE HEARTS
103. FOIL-COATED CHOCOLATE HEART
104. SKITTLES 105. FLYING SAUCERS
106. STRAWBERRY AND CREAM LOLLIES 107. TV SNACK MALT STICKS
108. SHERBET STRAWS 109. JAFFAS
110-113. FOIL-COVERED CHOCOLATE CARS, FROG, LADYBIRDS AND FISH
114. FRUIT MENTOS 115. TIM TAM FINGER BISCUITS 116. FRUIT TINGLES
117. MUSK LIFE SAVERS
118. ICE-CREAM WAFERS
119. LATTICE BISCUITS
120. ICE-CREAM CONES
121. CREAM-FILLED CHOCOLATE BISCUITS 122. FOIL-COVERED CHOCOLATE COINS 123. BOILED LOLLIES 124. CHOCOLATE-COATED LICORICE BULLETS 125. CLINKERS
126. CHOCOLATE MONTE BISCUIT
127. GIANT CHOCOLATE FRECKLE
128. LICORICE FRECKLE
129. BANANA RUNTS
130. BANANA LOLLIES
131. SHERBET TUBES

GLOSSARY

almonds

BLANCHED brown skins removed.

FLAKED paper-thin slices.

GROUND also called almond meal; nuts are powdered to a coarse flour texture for use in baking or as a thickening agent.

allspice

Also known as pimento or jamaican pepper; so-named because is tastes like a combination of nutmeg, cumin, clove and cinnamon – all spices.

baking paper

Also called parchment, silicon paper or non-stick baking paper; not to be confused with greaseproof or waxed paper. Used to line cake pans; also to make piping bags.

baking powder

A raising agent consisting mainly of two parts cream of tartar to one part bicarbonate of (baking) soda.

bicarbonate of soda

Also called baking soda; used as a leavening (rising) agent in baking.

biscuits

Also known as cookies.

butter

We use salted butter unless stated otherwise. Unsalted or 'sweet' butter has no added salt. 125g (4 ounces) is equal to 1 stick of butter.

buttermilk

Originally the term given to the slightly sour liquid left after butter was churned from cream, today it is made similarly to yoghurt. Sold in the refrigerated section in supermarkets.

cereal

COCO POPS chocolate-flavoured puffed rice.

FROOT LOOPS fruit-flavoured puffed rice.

PUFFED RICE gluten-free cereal made from whole brown rice grains.

RICE BUBBLES puffed rice product made with malt extract.

chocolate

CHOC BITS also called chocolate chips or chocolate morsels; available in milk, white and dark chocolate. Made of cocoa liquor, cocoa butter, sugar and an emulsifier; they hold their shape when baked, so are ideal for decorating.

CHOC MELTS discs of compounded milk, white or dark chocolate ideal for melting and moulding.

DARK COOKING also called compounded chocolate; made with vegetable oil. Good for cooking as it sets at room temperature.

DARK CHOCOLATE also called semi-sweet or luxury chocolate; made of a high percentage of cocoa liquor and cocoa butter, and little added sugar. Unless stated otherwise, we use dark eating chocolate in this book.

MILK CHOCOLATE most popular eating chocolate, mild and very sweet; similar in make-up to dark chocolate, with the difference being the addition of milk solids.

WHITE CHOCOLATE contains no cocoa solids but derives its sweet flavour from cocoa butter. Very sensitive to heat, so watch carefully.

chocolate hazelnut spread

We use Nutella; made of cocoa powder, hazelnuts, sugar and milk.

cinnamon

Available as sticks (quills) and ground into powder; one of the world's most common spices.

cocoa powder

Also called unsweetened cocoa; cocoa beans (cacao seeds) that have been fermented, roasted, shelled, then ground into a powder.

coconut

CREAM obtained commercially from the first pressing of the coconut flesh alone, without the addition of water; the second pressing (less rich) is sold as the milk. Available in cans and cartons at supermarkets.

DESICCATED concentrated, dried, unsweetened and finely shredded coconut flesh.

ESSENCE synthetically made from flavouring, oil and alcohol.

FLAKED dried flaked coconut flesh.

SHREDDED unsweetened thin strips of dried coconut flesh.

corn syrup

A sweet syrup made by heating cornstarch with water under pressure. It comes in light and dark types and is used in baking and confectionery making.

cornflour

Also also known as cornstarch; used as a thickening agent in cooking. Wheaten cornflour is made from wheat rather than corn (maize) and gives sponge cakes a lighter texture (due to the fact wheaten cornflour has some gluten).

cream

POURING also called pure cream. It has no additives, and contains a minimum fat content of 35%.
SOUR thick, commercially-cultured cream with a minimum fat content of 35%.
THICKENED a whipping cream that contains a thickener. Has a minimum fat content of 35%.

cream of tartar

The acid ingredient in baking powder; added to confectionery mixtures to help prevent sugar from crystallising. Keeps frosting creamy and improves volume when beating egg whites.

custard powder

Instant mixture used to make pouring custard; similar to North American instant pudding mixes.

eggs

We use large chicken eggs (60g) in our recipes unless stated otherwise. If a recipe calls for raw or barely cooked eggs, exercise caution if there is a salmonella problem in your area.

flour

BESAN also called chickpea flour or gram; made from ground chickpeas so is gluten-free and high in protein.
PLAIN an all-purpose white flour made from wheat.
RICE very fine, almost powdery, gluten-free flour; made from ground white rice.
SELF-RAISING plain or wholemeal all-purpose flour combined with baking powder in the proportion of 1 cup flour to 2 teaspoons baking powder. Also called self-rising flour.

food colouring

Vegetable-based substance available in liquid, paste or gel form. Used to change the colour of various foods

gelatine

A thickening agent. Available in sheet form (leaf gelatine) or as a powder – 3 teaspoons powdered gelatine (8g or one sachet) is roughly equivalent to four gelatine leaves.

ginger

CRYSTALLISED fresh ginger, cubed and preserved in syrup then coated in sugar.
FRESH also called green or root ginger; the thick gnarled root of a tropical plant.
GLACÉ fresh ginger root preserved in a sugar syrup; crystallised ginger can be substituted if rinsed with warm water and dried before using.
GROUND also known as powdered ginger; used as a flavouring in cakes and puddings but cannot be substituted for fresh ginger.
UNCRYSTALLISED or naked ginger; similar to crystallised ginger but without the sugar exterior.

glacé fruit

Fruit that has been preserved in sugar syrup.

glucose syrup

Also known as liquid glucose; a clear, thick liquid often made from wheat or corn starch.

golden syrup

A by-product of refined sugarcane; pure maple syrup or honey can be substituted.

honey

Honey sold in a squeezable container is not suitable for cooking as it is too runny.

ice-cream

Use good-quality ice-cream; ice-cream varieties differ from manufacturer to manufacturer depending on the quantities of air and fat incorporated into the mixture.

jam

Also called conserve or preserve.

lollies

Also called sweets or candy.

milk

We use full-cream homogenised milk unless stated otherwise.

milo
A chocolate malted sweetened milk drink base.

mixed fruit
Consists of a mixture of sultanas, raisins, currants, mixed peel and sometimes glacé cherries.

mixed peel
Candied citrus peel.

mixed spice
A classic mixture generally containing caraway, allspice, coriander, cumin, nutmeg and ginger, although cinnamon and other spices can be added.

modelling paste
Also known a BAS relief paste, gum paste, flower modelling paste and pastillage. Sets very hard, and is used to make all types of decorations for cakes. Work with small amounts at a time and keep the remaining paste airtight, wrapped in plastic wrap, to stop it from drying out. Models made from the paste will need anywhere from 1 hour to 2 days to dry completely before using. Colour modelling paste in the same way as ready-made icing.

nutmeg
A strong and very pungent spice ground from the dried nut of an evergreen tree native to Indonesia. Usually found ground, but the flavour is more intense from a whole nut, available from spice shops, so it's best to grate your own.

oil
COOKING SPRAY we use cholesterol-free spray made from canola oil.

VEGETABLE oils sourced from plants rather than animal fats.

pistachios
Pale green, delicately flavoured nut inside hard off-white shells. To peel, soak shelled nuts in boiling water about 5 minutes; drain, then pat dry with paper towel. Rub skins with cloth to peel.

popcorn
A variety of corn that is sold as kernels for popping, or can be bought ready popped.

poppy seeds
Small, dried, bluish-grey seeds of the poppy plant, with a crunchy texture and nutty flavour. Purchase whole or ground in most supermarkets.

ready-made white icing
Also called soft icing, ready-to-roll icing (RTR), fondant sugar, sugar paste, plastic icing and soft icing. It's sweet tasting, and has a dough-like consistency when kneaded. Available from the baking section in most supermarkets.

roasting/toasting
Roast nuts and dry coconut in the oven to restore their fresh flavour and release their aromatic essential oils. Spread evenly onto an oven tray and roast in a moderate oven (180°C/350°F) about 5 minutes. Desiccated coconut, pine nuts and sesame seeds roast more evenly if stirred over low heat in a heavy-based frying pan; their natural oils will help turn them golden brown. Remove immediately from the pan or tray, to stop them from burning.

star anise
A dried star-shaped pod with an astringent aniseed flavour.

sugar
BROWN a soft, finely granulated sugar retaining molasses for its characteristic colour and flavour.

CASTER also known as superfine or finely granulated table sugar. The fine crystals dissolve easily making it perfect for cakes and meringues.

DEMERARA small-grained golden-coloured crystal sugar.

ICING also called confectioners' or powdered sugar; granulated sugar is crushed together with a small amount of added cornflour.

PURE ICING also called confectioners' or powdered sugar; does not contain any cornflour (is gluten-free).

RAW natural brown granulated sugar.

VANILLA granulated or caster sugar flavoured with a vanilla bean; can be stored indefinitely.

WHITE a coarsely granulated table sugar; also called crystal sugar, unless stated otherwise.

sultanas
Also called golden raisins; dried seedless white grapes.

vanilla
BEAN dried, long, thin pod from a tropical golden orchid; the minuscule black seeds inside are used to impart a luscious vanilla flavour in baking and desserts.

EXTRACT beans soaked in alcohol. Essence is not a suitable substitute.

yoghurt
We use plain full-cream yoghurt in our recipes unless stated otherwise.

CONVERSION CHART

Measures

One Australian metric measuring cup holds approximately 250ml; one Australian metric tablespoon holds 20ml; one Australian metric teaspoon holds 5ml.

The difference between one country's measuring cups and another's is within a two- or three-teaspoon variance, and will not affect your cooking results. North America, New Zealand and the United Kingdom all use a 15ml tablespoon.

All cup and spoon measurements are level. The most accurate way of measuring dry ingredients is to weigh them. When measuring liquids, use a clear glass or plastic jug with metric markings.

We use large eggs with an average weight of 60g.

Dry measures

METRIC	IMPERIAL
15g	½oz
30g	1oz
60g	2oz
90g	3oz
125g	4oz (¼lb)
155g	5oz
185g	6oz
220g	7oz
250g	8oz (½lb)
280g	9oz
315g	10oz
345g	11oz
375g	12oz (¾lb)
410g	13oz
440g	14oz
470g	15oz
500g	16oz (1lb)
750g	24oz (1½lb)
1kg	32oz (2lb)

Oven temperatures

The oven temperatures in this book are for conventional ovens; if you have a fan-forced oven, decrease the temperature by 10-20 degrees.

	°C (CELSIUS)	°F (FAHRENHEIT)
Very slow	120	250
Slow	150	300
Moderately slow	160	325
Moderate	180	350
Moderately hot	200	400
Hot	220	425
Very hot	240	475

Liquid measures

METRIC	IMPERIAL
30ml	1 fluid oz
60ml	2 fluid oz
100ml	3 fluid oz
125ml	4 fluid oz
150ml	5 fluid oz (¼ pint)
190ml	6 fluid oz
250ml	8 fluid oz
300ml	10 fluid oz (½ pint)
500ml	16 fluid oz
600ml	20 fluid oz (1 pint)
1000ml (1 litre)	1¾ pints

Length measures

METRIC	IMPERIAL
3mm	⅛in
6mm	¼in
1cm	½in
2cm	¾in
2.5cm	1in
5cm	2in
6cm	2½in
8cm	3in
10cm	4in
13cm	5¼in
15cm	6in
18cm	7¼in
20cm	8in
23cm	9¼in
25cm	10in
28cm	11¼in
30cm	12in (1ft)

INDEX

THIS BOOK IS PUBLISHED IN 2015 BY OCTOPUS
PUBLISHING GROUP LIMITED BASED ON MATERIALS
LICENSED TO IT BY BAUER MEDIA BOOKS. AUSTRALIA
BAUER MEDIA BOOKS ARE PUBLISHED BY

Bauer Media Pty Limited
54 Park St, Sydney; GPO Box 4088,
Sydney, NSW 2001, Australia
phone (+61) 2 9282 8618; fax (+61) 2 9126 3702
www.awwcookbooks.com.au

BAUER MEDIA BOOKS

Publisher Jo Runciman
Editorial & food director Pamela Clark
Director of sales, marketing & rights Brian Cearnes
Art director Hannah Blackmore
Designer & illustrator Jeannel Cunanan
Junior editor Amy Bayliss
Food editor Emma Braz

Published and Distributed in the United Kingdom
by Octopus Publishing Group Limited,
Carmelite House, 50 Victoria Embankment, London EC4Y 0DZ.
phone (+44) (0) 207 632 5400; fax (+44) (0) 207 632 5405
info@octopusbooks.co.uk;
www.octopusbooks.co.uk

Printed in China with 1010 Printing Asia Limited.

International foreign language rights,
Brian Cearnes, Bauer Media Books
bcearnes@bauer-media.com.au

A catalogue record for this book is available
from the British Library.
ISBN: 978 1 74245 628 7 (paperback)

© Bauer Media Pty Ltd 2015
ABN 18 053 273 546
This publication is copyright. No part of it may be
reproduced or transmitted in any form without the